A Price Guide To

Rock & Roll

Collectibles

By
Greg Moore

Library of Congress Catalog Card Number 93-91812

ISBN 0-9639495-0-0

Printed in the United States of America

First Edition . . . November 1993
Second Edition . . . October 1994

Additional copies of this book may be ordered from:
Rock & Roll Collectibles
Attn: Greg Moore
P.O. Box 586
Aumsville, OR 97325

"When it ceases to be rare it loses its value."

Pat Boone
(1959)

TABLE OF CONTENTS

Preface.. i

Dedication.. iii

Acknowledgements iv

Introduction 1

How To Use This Book... 2

Collecting For Investment and Pleasure...................... 3

Values.. 4

Grading 5

Buying 6

Selling.. 7

Protecting Your Investment.. 8

Author's Note 9

Archies.. 11

Banana Splits 16

Beatles 19

Bee Gees 28

Pat Boone 30

California Raisins 32

Chipmunks.. 37

Donnie and Marie/Osmonds 42

Hammer 46

Michael Jackson/J-5 49

Josie and The Pussycats 52

Kiss 54

Madonna 58

Monkees.. 61

New Kids On The Block 65

Partridge Family.. 69

Elvis Presley 73

Rolling Stones 78

Bobby Sherman 80

Sonny and Cher 82

Vanilla Ice.. 84

Miscellaneous.. 86

Bibliography 95

Collecting anything is truly a matter of one's appreciation toward it. Without this appreciation we wouldn't have collectibles or a collectible audience. Collecting isn't for everyone. Some feel it's a waste of time, money and energy, many don't know how to perceive it at all. But, if it weren't for this consciousness there wouldn't be cherished items left to find for our collections. Prized items would be in short supply, the hunt would be no fun and life to the collector would be a bore.

Collecting is a challenge of finding items at reasonable rates before another collector does. A collector can spend as much or as little time and money as he or she desires. Once you start a collection or begin making money on collectibles, it's hard to stop. Every rock and roll collector has a specialty area he is particularly fond of. Some search for items of various groups like the Beatles, Kiss or Elvis, others cherish lunch kits, still others collect dolls or games. No matter what it is, some collector somewhere is after it. Collecting rock and roll merchandise is virtually endless. This book chronicles rock memorabilia from the 1950s to date and is as current, accurate and comprehensive as is believed possible

This book is dedicated to all of the music memorabilia enthusiasts and fanatics around the globe. Without them a book of this type could not exist. At a young age, most of these people probably spent a few hard-earned dollars on a rock and roll trinket only to lose it, throw it away or leave home without it. Then years later, with fond memories of childhood, a passion for toys or the enjoyment of a "fun" investment hobby, these same people spend entire paychecks and travel endlessly to regain these memories.

ACKNOWLEDGEMENTS

Many thanks to the kind and generous people who have contributed useful information and valuable time to this project. Without their unending support, this book would not be complete. Special thanks go to: my wife Pam for her endless hours of typing and understanding during this project, my kids Daphne and Tiffany who basically gave up their dad for nine months so this book could materialize, Fred and Jan Carlson for all their time and use of lunch boxes on picture day, Joe Hilton for the great Beatles pictures, Bob and Joan Gottuso (BOJO) for the use of their Monkees and Kiss pictures, Kip Siess for the use of the Elvis pictures, Larry De Angelo for the California Raisins pictures, Daniel Wachtenheim for the pictures and information on the Partridge Family, Jeff Kline the Splits and Chipmunks expert, Jerry Osborne for the use of the Elvis pictures and guidance, David Welch for his support and thoughts on this project, Roland Coover Jr. for his help in the cereal premium department, my patient photographers Pat Farrell and Jon Deming, Kevin Percha, Gary Conn Jr. and the folks at Kissaholics for the Kiss pictures, and Dick Pollard, Jon Shapiro, Laszlo Ficsor, David Marshall, and Judy at the Salem Library.

The world of collecting is a vast area. Within this area are millions of people collecting a huge array of items. During the past decade the popularity of character collectibles (rock and roll merchandise in particular) has found a new, captive audience. The majority of this audience is an aging Baby-Boomer generation that holds a place in its heart for childhood memories. The current collectible market is seeing a huge transition from more fundamental antique items (glass, china, furniture, etc. . .) to more colorful and collectible toy-related items. This change from a previous generation's collectibles to a more modern one has created a market frenzy for rock and roll merchandise.

Many of the items currently sought after are those of rock acts and rock-related Saturday morning TV shows. These items were originally targeted at a young audience. As this audience matures, childhood memories remain and create the desire for one to recapture them. Many rock and roll collectors begin with elaborate record collections and gradually move into the merchandise market. Though many types of rock collectibles exist, the ones with the most universal resale and collectible appeal are the toy-related items. Many collectors, realizing the values of merchandise created for the Beatles, Elvis and Kiss, are investing in the future by purchasing memorabilia of current musical acts such as Michael Jackson and The New Kids. Much of the more recent merchandise is already of value due to its limited production and/or scarcity.

Collectors of rock merchandise have been collecting items since the early Elvis years – nearly 40 years ago. The recent successful marketing of New Kids items shows us rock memorabilia is alive and well. With this continuing support by rock and roll fans, a stable collectible market should be active well into the future.

USING THIS BOOK

The single most important consideration of this book is that the price ranges of items cataloged should serve only as a guideline to approximate values. The value of any item is what someone is willing to pay. This pricing guide lists approximate values as per the current market prices on valuation of items from auctions, toy shows, trade periodicals and many other credible sources. However, due to supply and demand, fluctuation in the market and many other structuring factors, no price guide should be considered totally accurate.

All items listed in this book should be considered collectible. For the simple fact that many paper items such as books, posters, magazines etc. can be found in other publications, most have been omitted. Pin-back buttons and many clothing items (ie: t-shirts, hats) also have been excluded. This book's main focus is on the non-paper or clothing merchandise created for rock and roll related acts.

This book categorizes groups that merchandised the most items. You will find short histories of these groups followed by an alphabetical listing of the group's most common and most valuable merchandise. Also included are miscellaneous items from various other rock/pop related acts.

One final note is that many of the groups listed in this guide were not actual rock and roll groups but were, however, connected to rock music in some fashion and deserve mention here.

INVESTING IN COLLECTIBLES

When we invest in anything, be it real estate, stocks or even a soda pop, we do so because it brings a certain reward. There are two ways of looking at investing. The first is obviously for capital gain and the second is for pleasure. Collecting for pleasure is known as a hobby. Collecting for a profit is known as business. When investing in collectibles, more precisely character-related items, we capture the best of both worlds.

We collect because it brings a certain feeling of enjoyment, with which also comes a piece of American history that's better than money in the bank. By investing wisely and understanding trends, a person's investment is sure to appreciate steadily in value. Collecting is not a fad, it's big business and has been for years. The collectible toy market has boomed in recent years making many investors quite wealthy.

3

VALUES

It has been said, and is believed by the author, that the value of an item is what someone is willing to pay for it. This rule certainly applies in the world of collecting. However, one can't depend on this theory in terms of ultimate values. If we sell a certain item for more than a set price listed in a current book, we should feel lucky. Many items in the field of rock and roll collecting which were considered "junk" a few years ago are now demanding hundreds, even thousands of dollars. Much of the escalation in memorabilia pricing is due to publication of trade price guides, some high and some low. The difficult task for collectors has always been which source to believe. With fluctuating markets on the east and west coasts and especially in the midwest, a pricing game begins. It seems that to decide the value of an item, a person has to contact many sources. One thing is definite — it's always profitable if you can double your money, which is at the very least what many do when investing in the toy market.

Not only is it advantageous to buy items at relatively low prices but also to be selective when you buy. By keeping this and condition in mind it's hard to go wrong. Many items in this book have increased in value since this book has been published and continue to climb to all-time highs. Extreme care was used to obtain the most accurate information on the items in this book from credible sources around the states and the author believes the prices reflect a consensus of current market values.

With the small exception of a product's rarity, nothing is more important than its condition. The seasoned collector knows the importance of quality and will pass by most items that aren't in top condition. A beginning collector may purchase items in most any condition to start building a collection. As this collector becomes informed he/she may choose to upgrade a product's condition. This is a common practice. When doing this, however, be sure not to spend top dollar on less than mint or near mint items. Remember that nothing holds its value better than near perfect merchandise.

Grading categories are as follows:

Grade 10 = Mint: *Boxed, carded or packaged, perfect box or perfect card. No bends, tears, or fading. Brand new, store-bought items may not be mint due to handling or manufacturer flaws. A+*

Grade 9 = Near Mint/Excellent: *Extremely slight (usually shelf) wear. If boxed, item may have been removed and returned to box but not played with. Item has like new appearance. A*

Grade 8 = Fine: *Minor wear. Box or card may have slight wear or crease. Item still displays well with no major flaws. Grade 8 and above are the best to collect for resale investment value. B*

Grade 7 = Very Good: *Box, card or container may be damaged (ie: crushed corners, small tears, damaged cellophane) unboxed items show wear, some fading still complete but shows use. C*

Grade 6 Good: *Box is severely damaged, carded or container items taped, ripped or very faded if not missing all together. Loose items have scratches, worn paint, chips or decals missing. Avoid buying items in this or lower grade unless extremely rare. D*

Grade 5 Poor: *Item is missing box, card or container. Broken, damaged, or missing parts. Never buy items in this condition. F*

Remember, boxed items can usually account for 50-75% or more at of an item's value. The more an item changes hands, the more likely it is to be damaged. The best condition to buy items is in a Grade 8 or better condition. You will always be able to sell items that are in fine to mint condition faster than below grade 8. Some items can be purchased at reasonable prices due to slight damage and repaired to upgrade one or more categories. The values in this price guide is for merchandise in a grade 8 or better condition.

BUYING

There is nothing quite as exciting as finding an item you have been searching for and purchasing it for a reasonable (or better than) price. The "hunt" is what a collector lives for. If we were to find everything we were searching for in one place at one time it would spoil the element of the search. Several guidelines should be followed when buying. Maybe the single most important rule is if you want it, buy it. Chances are if you think about it too long it will be gone and may not surface again for years. Many a collector has experienced this disappointment. If you're running short on cash leave a deposit with the seller.

Many collectors seek certain specialty items (i.e.: lunch boxes, Beatles, comics) and search for just the ones desired. It is useful to ask sellers if they have what you may be looking for. Many sellers have more than they can display and have boxes of items hidden under tables. Also, by making contacts at shows you may stumble on a gold mine of merchandise by merely trading phone numbers.

When you come across an item you want examine it carefully. Many expensive mistakes are made when the buyer acts to hastily. Always buy items as complete and perfect as possible. Know your item's value when purchasing so you're not sorry later.

Be careful when purchasing paper items to check for flaws in condition and for resale value. Unlike toys, many paper items haven't held the test of time. Some of the best paper items to invest in are the cereal premiums and comic book send-always. These items are always more valuable with their original paper mailer or package.

When you are ready to make the purchase try to get your best possible price. This doesn't always mean offering less for an item. Always offer what you feel an item is worth to you especially if it's priced higher than you feel it should be. Try to put several items together for a better price if there are two or more items on a seller's table that you are interested in. If items of interest are unpriced, try to contain your excitement or you'll most likely pay more for them. If the seller has more than one of the item you want and they are affordable, buy them all for investment or for later trading. A last note on buying is to watch out for reproductions. Several Beatles items from the 1960s have been reproduced. Their authenticity is somewhat hard to recognize. Also many later issue Beatle items don't have the value of the vintage items but are nonetheless good additions for collections.

All sellers value things differently. Many feel they could or should get more for items than they are realistically worth. The seller may be asking an inflated price but, the buyer wants a deal. It has been said that an item's value is what someone is willing to pay for it. But, somewhere in the sales transaction there has to be a happy medium. In the end, it's usually the seller who backs down if he/she wants to make the sale. Trading items with other sellers is sometimes a useful way of reducing the costs of items you wish to purchase. By trading items that were purchased at a small cost and inflating the value in trade a person can end up with more cash in hand and ultimately get a better deal. Creative and effective trading takes time and skill to master.

As a seller it is wise to make as many contacts as you can in the market. By talking with people and keeping lists of what buyers are looking for, the seller has an edge. It's always easier to buy if you know what to sell and to whom. Many clubs are available for rock and roll enthusiasts and are good avenues for contacts whether buying or selling. The more contacts you make, the broader your scope of sale items becomes. With this also comes a better chance of finding the items you collect. There are several rules to consider before placing a price on an item. Using current publications may be useful in determining prices but they seldom are completely accurate. Contacting others in the field usually helps, but be careful. They may want the item themselves and offer you a price well below market value. Studying price guides and asking collectors/vendors of values is usually best. Several other factors should come into play when determining a value or sales price. They are as follows:

1. Rarity — were limited amounts made.

2. Desirability — toys vs paper items.

3. Popularity — how many remember the item.

4. Availability — how often do you see it.

5. Condition — how clean is it.

6. Age — how old is it (not always a factor).

7. Multi interest — how many different groups of collectors would be interested.

PROTECTING YOUR INVESTMENT——

There is really nothing more disappointing than damaging an item that is special to you. Care should be taken to protect your collection. Current pictures and video tape should be taken and submitted with appraisal to your insurance company if you feel that your collection warrants replacement coverage. Many insurance companies have to write special policies to cover collectibles but, the price of these policies is relatively small compared with the values of some collections. All valuable collections are best secured under lock and key for further safety.

Strong, supported shelves should be used when displaying heavy items and always be careful when stacking things. Damage from earthquakes, kids or clumsy elbows can be avoided by using sticky foam square holders to secure items in place. However, be careful when using them so as not to damage items such as boxed, paper or painted ones.

Sunlight, humidity and dust are also factors to consider when displaying items. All can damage items if care is not taken. Paper items should always be wrapped in plastic cellophane or mylar covers. Paper items are especially vulnerable to damage from fading, curling or worse. Never attach paper items to a wall with pins or staples; holes greatly detract from a paper item's value.

When cleaning metal items, never submerge in water. Water causes rust which ruins items. Hinges on lunch boxes for example don't usually dry fast enough to avoid rusting. Cleaning of lunch kits – metal, vinyl or plastic – is best done selectively using a small amount of a slightly abrasive liquid cleaner with water, rubbing lightly and drying immediately. Gum from labels can be removed with lighter fluid, but always use caution.

With a little care and protection, your collection should be enjoyed and grow in value indefinitely.

Through searching, collecting and appreciating rock and roll memorabilia, nothing has been as rewarding as the people I've met and the friends I've made. Collectors are a special breed of people. Most I've met are extremely friendly, exciting people who could talk about collecting for hours. Collecting adds pleasure and enrichment to our lives. The people we meet simply add to the joy of it all.

Some items listed in this book are not licensed but, due to their collective interest, deserve mention. Also, there are many specialty books written on such groups as The Beatles and Elvis. These publications have a more complete listing of these groups than space allows here. It is impossible to know of and list all rock and roll merchandise made. Special care has been taken to consult expert sources in their fields for this book and the best care has been made to assure prices listed are accurate in today's market. But, as previously mentioned, prices here should serve only as a guide.

What better figure, or group, to transform from comic book legend to rock and roll Star/Group then Archie Andrews and his singing group, the Archies. Archie first began life in December 1941 in the 22nd issue of MLJ's PEP Comics by creator Bob Montana. Through time the Archie Comic became the most famous comic in the world selling one million copies per month at its peak in 1969.

Archie and his pals Jughead Jones, Betty Cooper, Veronica Lodge, Reggie Mantle and a host of others are truly a part of America's Nostalgic history.

The Archie's Rock group was created by Don Kirshner (Monkee's Producer) as a bubble gum studio group. Kirshner's intent was to create top-selling songs. The group produced such memorable hits as "Sugar Sugar" and "Jingle Jangle," each selling a million copies in 1969.

Along with the music, a series of animated TV shows ran beginning with the Archie Show that aired in September of 1968. The show was followed by five more Archie series on CBS that ran through September of 1976. The Archie series spawned other memorable comic figures such as Josie and Sabrina.

The comics sold millions before the singing group was created in 1968. With the success of the group's singles, came lots of toys and merchandise connecting the Archies to rock and roll. Archie memorabilia (mainly toys) is rapidly decreasing from circulation. Some items have enjoyed tremendous increases in value within the past few years (like the 1975 Marx dolls). Some of the most valuable of Archie memorabilia are the more scarce comics that fetch up to $600.00. Though the earlier comics didn't relate Archie to Rock and Roll, they are still certainly part of Archie's vast array of collectibles. In general, Archie merchandise for the rock era is some of the most colorful and affordable merchandise today. The Archie toys (pre-1980) are especially worthy of investment.

Archie Kit

Beanie

Bubble Funnies

Carry Case

Marx Doll

Presents Doll

ARCHIES KIT	1991	50th anniversary pak kit includes: pen, 2″x2″ button, notepad, membership card	20-25
BEANIE	1968	cereal premium felt (Jughead)	50-80
BUBBLE FUNNIES	1981	AMURAL 2 1/4″ x 3 1/2″ each	5-8
BUTTON MAKING SET	1969		50-75
BUBBLE GUM CARDS	1992	SKYBOX	card .10-.15
		set of 120	set 12-15
		hologram set(4)	22-25
		sendaway hologram	10-12
CARRY CASE	1975	MARX doll tote	45-65
CARS	1988	MCDONALDS	set of 6 each 3-5
			set 15-20
			box only 5-8
	1991	BURGER KING	set of 4 each 2-3
			set 5-8
COLORING BOOK	1972	WHITMAN Jughead	10-15
DOLLS	1975	MARX 8″	set of 4 each 40-60
	1977	MATTEL 8″	set of 5 each 25-35
	1987	PRESENTS 18″	set of 4 each 25-35
	1989	JESCO 6″ (sendaway)	set of 5 ea. 10-15
DRUM	1969	EMENFE	55-75
FACE PUPPET		5″ Archie foam rubber	10-15
FUZZY FACE	1991	JARU with candy	3-5
GAME	1987	JARU no candy	3-5
GAMES	1963	HASBRO "Archie Fun Game"	50-75
	1969	WHITMAN "Archie"	20-40
HAIR DRYER	1986	JARU	3-5

Dome Lunch Box

Lunch Box and Thermos

Marx Jalopy

Hair Dryer

Junior Shaver

Money Set

Fuzzy Face Game

HALLOWEEN COSTUME	1969	BEN COOPER		25-40
JALOPY	1975	MARX 12″ plastic		50-75
	1975	LJN 2 1/2″ metal		20-40
JELLY GLASSES	1971	WELCHES	set of 6 each	4-6
	1973	WELCHES	set of 6 each	4-6
			set in box	60-75
JUNIOR SHAVER KIT	1986	JARU Jughead		3-5
LOONIES	1986	JARU plastic bubbles & straws		3-5
LUNCH BOXES	1969	ALADDIN steel		50-90
	1991	METRO KANE (plastic dome)		30-45
MODEL KIT	1968	AURORA (Jalopy)		100-125
MONEY SET	1991	JARU		3-5
PACHINKO GAME	1991	JARU		3-5
PAPER DOLLS	1969	WHITMAN		15-25
	1969	WHITMAN (boxed)		25-35
PENCIL BY NUMBERS	1987	ART AWARD		15-20
PHONE SET	1987	JARU		3-5
POCKET PUZZLE	1960'S	JAYMAR		10-15

Drum

Face Puppet

Phone Set

Loonies

Pachinko Game

Whitman's Archie Game

Paper Dolls

Pencil by Number Set

Viewmaster

Puffy Stickers

Trace and Color Set

Watch

POPPERS	1969	3″ plastic (premium)	set of 3 ea. 25-30
PUFFY STICKERS	1982	OUR WAY	8-15
PURSE	1986	JARU	10-15
PUZZLES	1972	WHITMAN frame tray	ea. 10-15
			boxed set of 4 70-90
	1969	JAYMAR jigsaw	30-40
	1988	JAYMAR jigsaw	5-10
RECORDS	1969	cut outs from cereal box	ea. 6-10
RING TOSS	1987	JARU	3-5
RUB-ONS	1969	SUGAR RICE CEREAL	10-15
SKIN RUB-ONS	1969	CRISPY CRITTERS CEREAL	10-15
SLIDE VIEWER	1973	KENNER filmstrip	10-15
SQUIRT PEN	1987	JARU	5-8
STATIONARY	1960'S	7 1/2″ x 9 1/2″	40-50
STENCIL SET	1986	JARU	5-8
STICKERS	1989	DIAMOND	each .20-.25
		set of 180	set 30-35
			wrapper .20-.25
STICKER ALBUM	1989	DIAMOND	5-8

Jelly Glasses

Whitman Puzzle Set

Jaymar Puzzle

Purse

Ring Toss

Squirt Pen

Stencil Set

TATTOOS	1969	TOPPS set of 16	sheet 8-12 wrapper 20-25
THERMOS	1969	ALADDIN	plastic 15-30
TRANSFER BOOK	1977	GOLDEN iron ons	15-20
TRACE AND COLOR	1987	JARU	5-8
WATCH	1989	CHEVAL LED has changeable faces	20-30
VIEWMASTER	1975	GAF	20-30

Records

Jesco Doll Set

McDonalds Car Set

Burger King Car Set

BANANA SPLITS

Tra-la-la Tra-la-la-la was what you heard when you tuned into NBC-TV Saturday mornings from September 7, 1968 through September 5, 1970. The Banana Splits' Adventure Hour was a successful rock and roll show featuring four costumed figures dressed as animals that performed skits in their playhouse. The show was sponsored by Kellogs and offered several mail-in premiums including a fan club, mug and bowl set and records. This colorful action series by Hanna Barbera was targeted at the under 10-year-old audience.

The animals were Fleegle - dog, Drooper - lion, Bingo - gorilla and Snorky an elephant. The Splits, unlike the more abrasive music and acts that the kids' teen brothers and sisters followed, were pure, clean fun. They bumbled around their playhouse, played rock and roll songs and promoted such practices as helping mom and dad, learning at school, taking out the garbage, and cleaning up. It truly was a milestone for Hanna Barbera to include children in rock and roll but not deviate from moral guidelines.

Banana Splits memorabilia is becoming extremely difficult to find. Their colorful toys have long been sought after by rock and roll and toy collectors alike. All Splits' toys are a good investment to purchase in most any condition. Since most of these items were played with by children years ago, finding Splits items in excellent to mint condition is extremely rare. This makes even the slightest grading improvement (say from fine condition, Grade 7 to an excellent condition, Grade 8) extremely favorable. Though some items are more scarce, the Banana Splits' vinyl lunch box continues to be the most sought after and highest priced item merchandised by the group. As an example of this condition value, the lunch box alone (no thermos) with a grading of 7 is valued at about $175.00-200.00. One step higher (Grade 8) and the box value increases to $275.00-300.00.

BANANA BAND	1973	LARAMI horn, sax & mouth harp	45-55	
COLORING BOOK	1969	WHITMAN paint & color book	25-35	
COMICS		GOLD KEY	number 1 15-20	
			all others 3-10	
CUPS		plastic 7-11	set of 4 ea. 15-20	
		paper party cups	9oz. ea. 5-10	
			sealed pack 30-40	
DOLLS	1969	pillow type cereal giveaway	ea. 30-40	
		in plastic mailer	65-85	
	1969	HASBRO rubber doll 4″ rubber		
		carded or boxed	75-100	
		stuffed doll large	each 100-150	
		SUTTON doll plastic small		
		w/glasses	ea. 60-75	
		SUTTON doll stuffed small		
		w/color photo of group tag	75-85	
ERASERS	1968	cereal premium	set of4 each 40-50	
FAN CLUB KIT	1968	Includes: pennant, membership card,		
		decoder, handbook, sticker, certif.		
		in original mailer	90-130	
FLUTE SET	1973	LARAMI carded	35-45	
FIGURE		Fleegle ceramic 12″	75-100	
GAME	1969	HASBRO recording studio fun	100-125	
HALLOWEEN COSTUME	1968	BEN COOPER	125-150	
HARMONICA	1973	LARAMI small	30-45	
KUT-UP KIT	1973	LARAMI carded	20-30	
LUNCH BOX	1969	THERMOS vinyl	300-400	
MODEL KIT	1968	AURORA banana buggy	175-225	
MUG AND BOWL SET	1969	cereal premium set w/mailer	85-100	
		mug	20-25	
		bowl	20-25	
NUMBERED PENCIL COLOR SET	1969	HASBRO	75-95	
PAINT BY NUMBER	1969	HASBRO	95-125	
POST CARD		large 3-D	20-30	

Comics

Party Cup

Halloween Costume

Pillow Dolls

Fan Club Kit

Kut-up Kit

Mug and Bowl Set

Record

PRINTING SET	1970	plastic	40-60
PUZZLES	1969	WHITMAN frame tray	each 30-40
			boxed set 75-110
	1969	WHITMAN jigsaw 100pcs.	50-60
RECORDS	1968	DECCA "WERE" The Banana Splits	60-70
	1969	sendaway 2diff. 45rpm	25-30
RINGS		Canadian	each 25-45
SCHOOL TABLET	1968	WESTAB 8″ x10″	20-35
SHEETING PUPPETS		one of each character cereal premium	each 15-20
SLIDE PUZZLE		ROALEX	pkg. 75-100
STAND-UP RUB ON SET	1969	HASBRO	75-100
STICH-A-STORY SET	1969	HASBRO	65-85
SWITCH PLATE	1970	on card	65-75
TABLE CLOTH	1969	BEACH PRODUCTS paper sealed	30-45
TALKING TELEPHONE	1969	HASBRO	150-175
TAMBOURINE	1973	LARAMI small or large each	30-40
TATTOOS		small various types	each 10-15
THERMOS	1969	THERMOS metal	75-100
TOTEM	1969	pez type candy dispenser	100-175
VIEWMASTER	1970	GAF	40-50

School Tablet

Lunch Box and Thermos

Frame Tray Puzzles

Many will agree that with the death of John Kennedy came the birth of the Beatles. Simply put America was depressed, vulnerable and felt as if she had hit rock bottom due to this and other worldly events of the time. America was ready for a ray of hope, something new. Musically it had been two years since Elvis Presley had had a number one hit. Pat Boone, Ricky Nelson and Fats Domino had all become yesterdays hit makers. Rock music was in a slump. A change was eminent. The timing for the Beatles was perfect. Certainly, with their introduction came the beginning of a new era. But with this also came, for the first time, a band where each member was a star in the show and where the band's material was (for the most part) their own.

After Ed Sullivan (February 9, 1964), the Beatles soared in popularity unequaled to this day by any group. They sold records (and lots of them), made movies, changed our hair style and created memorabilia of most everything imaginable. Their music changed the way we think of rock and roll. Rock became smoother, more refined and we grew right along with it. On September 25, 1965 the Beatles Animated Cartoon series aired on ABC, another first in Rock history. The show ran through September 7, 1969 and had a total of 52 episodes. Two songs were featured on each of the shows, which is one reason so many watched. The show helped pave the way for others in animated form like The Jackson 5 and The Osmonds.

Now let's consider for a moment the immense possibilities this phenomenon had. You have a captive audience; hungry for anything that relates to its favorite band; most of this audience was teenaged or younger. What's next? Merchandise. And merchandise it was and continues to be. It is virtually impossible to know exactly how many different Beatles' items were produced, both licensed or counterfeit. But what we do know is how valuable most of these items are today. Most all non-paper items (toys for the most part) dated 1960s by NEMS or the Beatles own SELTAEB are continuing to demand top dollar at auctions and collectors shows. Many of these items have doubled in value within just the past few years. This makes collecting Beatles' memorabilia a blue chip investment. This merchandise is truly the bankable type that will hold the test of time for the obvious reason of the bands popularity, the items' scarcity, and the wants of collectors. The following list is merely a smattering of the more common Beatle items from the hundreds available.

Apron

Booty Bag/Bamboo Plate/Balloon

Brunch Bag/Dairy and Display Box/Coloring Book/Comb

Airflite Bags

Book Covers/Ball/Banjo

Beatles Forever Dolls

AIRFLITE BAG	1964	NEMS round or square		500-700
APRON	1964	black/white or red/white		250-400
ASSIGNMENT BOOK	1964	SELECT-O-PAK		150-200
BAG (BOOTIE)	1964	plastic with drawstring		100-150
BALL	1964	NEMS 8″ white		300-450
		NEMS 9″ black		400-550
		NEMS 14″ playball		200-350
BALLOON	1964	UNITED IND. assorted colors		50-75
BAMBOO TRAY	1964	SPECIALIST various sizes		60-125
BANJO	1964	MASTRO		800-1000
BEACH TOWEL	1965	NEMS 34″ X 56″		100-150
BELT	1964	leather, coin size faces		50-75
BINDER	1964	NEMS various colors		90-115
BONGOS	1964	MASTRO		750-1000
BOOK COVERS	1964	black and white pictures		15-20
		package of 7		50-85
BRACELETS	1964	RANDALL OR U.S. CERAMIC CO.		90-150
BRIEF COVER	1964	SELECT-O-PAK		250-300
BRUNCH BAG	1966	ALADDIN blue vinyl		350-450
CAKE DECORATIONS		2″ plastic (blue)		20-30 set
		2 1/2″ plastic (grey)		30-40 set
		other types		15-25 set
		boxed		add 10-15
CALENDER BANK		"make a date with the Beatles"		300-375
CANDY BOXES		set of 4		each 50-75
				set 200-265

Cake Decorations: 4 different Pauls

*Dell Comic/Cartoon Kit/Ringo Cap/
Candy Boxes/Coin Holder/Inflatable Dolls*

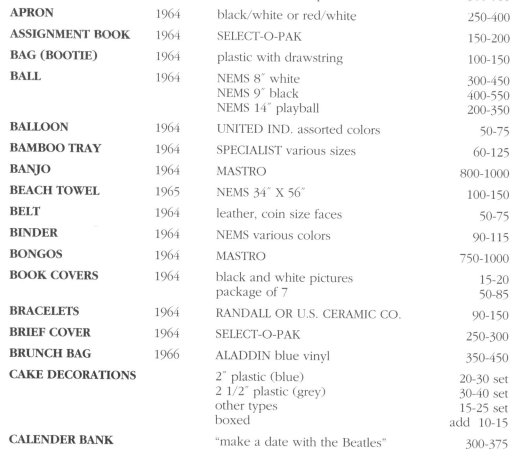

*Disc-Go-Case/Large and Small
Record Case/Record Carrier*

Sgt. Pepper Dolls

Remco Dolls

Game

*Yeah Yeah Guitar/Beatles Guitar/
Four Pop Guitar/Junior Guitar*

First Series Gum Cards

CAP		black leather tag says "Ringo"	85-150
		corduroy or cloth	50-100
CARTOON KIT	1966	NEMS (colorforms)	375-450
CLUTCH PURSE	1964	DAME	250-300
COIN	1964	commemorating tour	15-25
COIN HOLDER	1964		ea. 30-45
COLORING BOOK	1964	SAALFIELD	50-70
COMB	1964	LIDO 12″ various colors	50-75
COMIC	1964	DELL comic	100-135
		MARVEL OR DC comic	40-60
COMPACT	1964	photo on lid Gold case	225-425
DIARY	1965	vinyl	30-50
		display box	100-150
DISK-GO-CASE	1966	NEMS record carrier each	80-150
		various colors	
DOLLS	1987	Beatles forever series	35-50 ea.
		APPLAUSE 20″ cloth	125-200 set
	1964	bobbing heads	ea. 75-125
		carmascot 8″ plaster boxed	set 475-550
	1966	inflatable	ea. 30-65
		NEMS 15″ vinyl	set 85-110
		sealed	100-175
	1980	John Lennon figural radio	60-110
		10″ base has Radio	
	1964	REMCO boxed	ea. 150-200
		4″ rubber loose	40-75
		no instr.	30-45
		Note: John and George valued about 10% higher	
	1988	APPLAUSE 20″ cloth	ea. 35-50
		Sgt. Pepper Series	set 125-200

*Mug/Assorted Glasses/Cup/Tumbler/
Guitar String/Swingers Music Set/Compact*

*Bank/Talc/Gum Card Display Box/Hair Spray/
Hummer/Wallet/Harmonica/Playing Cards*

Nylon Headband/Back and Front

Kaboodle Kit

Shoes/Lampshade/Pen/Pen Holder

Hanger/Hat, Beach Type

Lunch Box with Thermos

Jigsaw Puzzzle, 1991

DRUMS		MASTRO OR SELCO 4 variations	ea.400-600
GAME	1964	MILTON BRADLEY Flip your wig	75-150
GLASSES	1964	clear 5 variations	each 85-100
			set 425-450
GUITARS		BEATLEIST GUITAR	600-700
		BIG SIX	500-600
		POP FOUR GUITAR	700-900
		JUNIOR GUITAR	400-500
		NEW BEAT	500-600
		NEW SOUND	500-600
		RED JET GUITAR	1,200-1,400
		YEAH YEAH GUITAR	1,200-1,500
GUITAR STRING	1964	HOFNER	85-155
GUM CARDS	1964	TOPPS card	1.50-2.00
		series 1 set of 60 (B&W)	set 150-175
			pack 30-45
			wrapper 25-30
			display box 75-125
		series 2 set of 55 (B&W)	card 1.50-2.00
			set 130-170
			pack 30-45
			wrapper 25-30
			display box 75-125
		series 3 set of 50 (B&W)	card 1.50-2.00
			set 125-175
			pack 30-45
			wrapper 25-30
			display box 75-125
		series 4 set of 64	card 1.50-2.00
			set 150-175
			pack 30-45
			wrapper 25-30
			display box 75-125

Ice Cream Wrapper/Model Kits

Paint Set

Pillows/Punch Out Portraits/Pennant

GUM CARDS, cont.

	diary series set of 60		card 1.50-2.00
			set 150-175
			pack 30-45
			wrapper 25-30
			display box 75-125
	A Hard Days Night series		card 1.50-2.00
			set of 55
			set 150-175
			pack 30-45
			wrapper 25-30
			display box 75-125

Record Player

HAIRBOWS		BURLINGTON various colors	175-275
HAIR BRUSH	1964	red,white or blue	25-30
HAIR GROWING TOY	1964	MERIT	200-275
HAIR POMADE	1964	PHILLIPINES packet	50-60
		display box	500-550
HAIR SPRAY	1964	NEMS Bronson	600-800
HANDBAGS	1964	DAME	325-450
HALLOWEEN COSTUMES	1964	BEN COOPER boxed	350-450
HANGERS	1967	SANDERS ENT.	ea. 75-125
HARMONICA	1964	HOHNER 2 types	boxed 100-200
			carded 150-300
HATS	1964	various styles	75-125
HEAD BANDS	1964	Betterwear band (nylon)	40-60
		Burlington band (cloth)	100-150
HEADPHONES	1964	KOSS	600-900
HUMMER	1964	NEMS	85-125
ICE CREAM WRAPPER	1964	COUNTRY CLUB ICE CREAM CO.	20-30
IRISH LINEN	1964	VISTER 18″ x 28″	75-150
KABOODLE KIT	1964	STD. PLASTIC 8 colors	700-1,000
KEYCHAINS	1964	NEMS black/white picture	50-85
		black plastic record 3″ concert promo.	15-20
LAMPS/SHADES	1964	English unknown maker	500-700
LICORICE CANDY RECORDS	1964	wrapper candy and photo	90-135
		wrapper and insert	75-110
		display box	100-175
LUNCH BOX	1965	ALADDIN blue steel	225-400

Rings

Dimensionals, Watercolors Lg/Sm

Scarf/Clutch Purses/Wig/Scrapbook

Pouch/Brief Cover/School Report Cover/Assignment Book

School Bag/Perfume

Soakies and Stamps

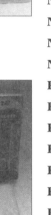

*Shoulder Bag/Halloween
Costume/Handbags*

Yellow Submarine Clock and Box

Yellow Submarine Puzzle (large)

Item	Year	Description	Price
LUX SOAP BOX		inflatable doll promo	200-250
MEGAPHONE	1964	NEMS 8″ white	200-300
MODEL KITS	1964	REVELL George or John	175-250
		Paul or Ringo	150-225
		Box only	50-75
MUGS		4″ ceramic (English)	100-135
		4″ ceramic NEMS	100-135
NAPKINS	1963	foreign	ea. 30-40
NECKLACES		RANDALL OR US CERAMIC CO.	75-110
NOTEBOOK	1964	WESTAB 2 styles	ea. 125-175
NYLONS	1964	BALLITZ OR CAREFREE	95-125
PAINT SET	1964	ARTISTIC CREATIONS	400-550
PEN HOLDER	1964	U.S. CERAMIC CO.	350-400
PENS	1964	RANDALL	75-125
PERFUME	1963	U.K.	2000-2300
PENCIL CASE	1964	various colors B&W photo	75-120
PENNANTS		various colors and styles	30-75
PILLOWS	1964	3 variations	100-150
PLAKS	1964	TOPPS	card 10-15
			set 600-800
			pack 100-125
			wrapper 25-30
			display box 75-125
PLAYING CARDS	1964	red box color cards 2 decks	150-250
		single deck	75-175
PORTRAITS	1964	various styles/makers	55-80
POUCH	1964	SELECT-O-PAC	250-300
PUNCH-OUT PORTRAITS	1964	WHITMAN	50-75
PUZZLES	1991	GOLDEN jigsaw	10-12
	1970s	assorted jigsaw	15-20
	1960s	foreign jigsaw 340 pcs.	125-225
RECORD CARRIER	1964		200-250
RECORD CASE	1964	AIRFLITE	small 150-250
			large 225-325
RECORD PLAYER	1964	NEMS photo of group	1,500-2,000
RINGS	1964	flasher ring - colored plastic	ea 5-10
		set of four	20-40
RUG	1964	21″ X 35″ four faces woven	325-400
SCARF		DAME	small 30-90
			large 45-100
SCHOOL BAG	1964	canadian	1200-1500
SCHOOL REPORT COVERS	1964	SELECT O PAK	125-200
SCRAPBOOK	1964	WHITMAN	65-100
SHOES	1964	WING DING low style boxed	400-550
		high top boxed	450-600
		box only	60-125
SHOULDER BAG	1964	9″ x 11″ vinyl w/strap ast.colors	275-375

SKATEBOARD	1964	19″ x 6″ photo and logo loose boxed	500-800 1200-1500
SOAKIES	1965	COLGATE Paul or Ring only boxed	ea. 65-85 200-250
STAMPS	1964	HALLMARK 100 stamps	25-50
SUNGLASSES	1964	BUCHMANN	50-100
SWINGERS MUSIC SET		3″ colored plastic carded 3″ painted fugures boxed 4″ plastic nodders carded	70-90 100-135 70-90
TALCUM POWDER	1964	MARGO OF MAYFAIR 7″ tin	300-400
THERMOS	1965	ALADDIN blue steel	75-155
TIE TACK	1964	NEMS each Beatle Guitar pin	30-60 40-70
TILE	1964	6″ x 6″ ceramic various	ea. 75-175
TRAY	1964	13″ x 13″ tin sticker on back	40-55
TUMBLER	1964	BURRITE plastic w/ paper insert	55-75
WALLETS	1964	STD. PLASTICS various colors	125-250
WALLPAPER	1964	roll	200-250
WIG	1964	LOWELL TOY	60-100

YELLOW SUBMARINE MERCHANDISE

ALARM CLOCK	1968	SHEFFIELD boxed loose	900-1100 300-400
BANKS	1968	PRIDE CREATIONS each Beatle	300-400 set 1200-1500
BINDER	1968	VERNON ROYAL 3 ring type	200-300
BULLETIN BOARD	1968	UNICORN CREATIONS 28″ X 7″ various styles	50-85
CANDY CIGARETTES	1968	PRIMROSE CONFECTIONARY	175-210
CANDLE	1968	CONCEPT DEVELOPMENT	450-600
COASTERS	1968	sealed pack	100-150
COMIC BOOK	1968	GOLD KEY	100-125
DESK SET	1968	A & M LEATHER LINE	700-750
DIMENTIONALS	1968	CRAFT MASTER pkged	150-250
HALLOWEEN COSTUMES	1968	COLLEGVILLE boxed	140-240

Yellow Submarine Scrapbook/ Photo Albums (Large and small)/Desk Set

Yellow Submarine Lunch Box with Thermos

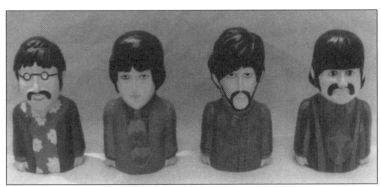

Yellow Submarine Banks

Yellow Submarine Mobile/Binder/Stationery/Comic/ Notebook (large)

HANGERS	1968	16″ cardboard four Beatles	ea. 65-95
KEYCHAIN	1968	PRIDE CREATIONS rectangular set of 5	60-100
		round set of 6	60-100
LUNCH BOX	1968	THERMOS steel	235-350
MOBILE	1968	SUNSHINE ART various loose	40-75
		sealed	100-175
MODEL KIT	1968	MPC boxed	150-300
		box only	50-75
NOTE BOOK	1968	KING FEATURES	small 45-75
			large 55-135
PENCIL HOLDER	1968		300-350
PHOTO ALBUM	1968	A & M LEATHERLINE	small 150-200
			large 250-325
POP-OUT ART DECORATIONS	1968		20-30
POSTER PUT ONS	1968	CRAFTMASTER	boxed 100-150
PUZZLES	1968	JAYMAR 5″ X 7″ small	45-95
		8″ X 9″ medium	55-110
		12″ X 12″ large	65-125
RUB-ONS	1968	Wheat or Rice Honeys	each 15-20
SCRAPBOOK	1968	A & M LEATHERLINE	575-600
STATIONERY	1968	UNICORN CREATIONS sealed	75-125
STICK-ONS	1968	DAL MFG. CO. various	each 35-75
SWITCH PLATE COVERS	1968	DAL MFG. CO. various	30-50
THERMOS	1968	THERMOS metal	75-155
WALL HANGER	1968	MPC	190-250
WATER COLORS	1968	CRAFT MASTER	small 90-175
			large 125-175
WRISTWATCH	1968	SHEFFIELD	800-1000
YELLOW SUB TOY	1968	CORGI 6″ metal	loose 100-150
			boxed 250-350

Yellow Submarine Corgi Toy/Party Coasters/Wrist Watch/Candy Cigarettes/Candle

Yellow Submarine Key Chain Sets

During the late 1960s and 1970s many Beatle items were reproduced or counterfeited. Though these items aren't considered "Genuine" to the serious Beatle collector, many consider them welcome additions to their collections. The list below is of the most popularly known Beatle "Fakes."

BANDAGE DISPENSER	HELP! white plastic	20-30
BANK	plastic 4″ round various colors	12-20
BUBBLES	8oz. Beatles bubbles	40-50
CALENDER BANK	"make a date with" 5″ x5″ plastic	30-40
CHANGE PURSE	small square vinyl assorted colors	15-25
DOLLS	nodder type 4″ plastic	set 10-15
ERASER	school type pictures Beatles	5-10
HAIRBRUSH	pictures faces left to right assorted colors	15-25
KNIFE	folding pocket type	5-15
PEN HOLDER	black pen in white square holder	30-40
PENCIL CASE	vinyl various colors	20-25
PENCILS	one of each Beatle	set 20-30
PUZZLE	frame tray black and white	25-35
RULER	plastic various colors	15-20
SCARF	various types	15-20
SLIDE PUZZLE	3″ x 3 1/2″ black and white plastic	20-30
THERMOMETER	2 1/2″ x 7″ tin fan club	30-35
TRAY	13″ x 13″ tin tea tray	30-45
WHISTLE	HELP! plastic	20-25
WOODEN NICKEL	pictures all 4 Beatles	5-10

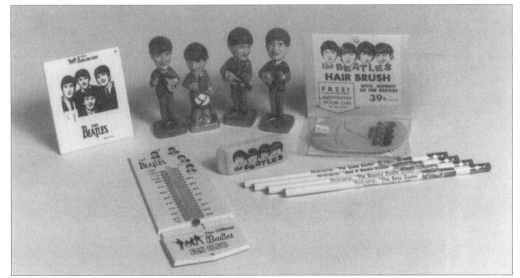

Counterfeit Items: Slide Puzzle/Nodders/Hairbrush/Thermometer/Eraser/Pencils

Counterfeit Items: Round Bank/Make A Date with Bank/Bubbles/Help Whistle and Band Aid Dispenser/Wooden Nickel/Knife/Scarf

BEE GEES

Five members originally made up the Bee Gees when they made their debut in America. Two members were forgotten and the three brothers made history. The Bee Gees enjoyed success in the late 1960s and 1970s with a string of hits. But it wasn't until the release of the sound track to the movie Saturday Night Fever in 1977 that the group rocketed to superstar status. Though many groups tried, the Bee Gees were then undisputed kings of the disco era, and the "fever" sound track and film were to be known as the plateau of the disco movement.

Disco was the creation of fast beating music, lights, glittered clothes and above all DANCE. Nightclubs popped up across the nation. Disco dance lessons were taught, dance clothes sold and merchandise was created to accommodate the fad. Historically, disco was a fusion of what pop music had turned into, a metamorphosis through time. The important factor is that, for the first time dance played a major role in music. This would be the founding and stepping stone for most pop music.

Andy Gibb was another important player in this era and as a brother of the Bee Gees deserves mention here. Andy enjoyed super stardom as a solo act and had five gold hits, three of which were Number one singles.

Andy, unlike his brothers, chose slower songs without the fast pace disco beat for his fans and it worked. Andy was also considered a sex symbol among his young audience.

The merchandise issued for the Bee Gees and Andy is for the most part still available at very reasonable prices. But after his death in 1987 the Andy Gibb doll doubled in price. The Bee Gees' lunch boxes have increased sharply in value also. This increase, however, has been fueled mainly by the increasing interest in metal lunch boxes by collectors. Other Bee Gee merchandise represents not only a group, but the era of disco music. For this reason more than just Rock and Roll collectors are interested in their merchandise.

BELT BUCKLE	1970s	brass with Bee Gee logo		10-20
DOLL	1979	IDEAL Andy Gibb 7″ boxed		30-40
GLASS	1979	Bee Gees logo		15-18
LUNCH BOXES	1978	THERMOS Barry	steel	50-60
	1978	THERMOS Maurice	steel	45-55
	1978	THERMOS Robin	steel	45-55
	1978	THERMOS Bee Gees	plastic	20-25
MICROPHONE AND AMP	1979			30-50
PHONOGRAPH	1979	IMAGE FACT. Bee Gees		30-50
POSTERS	1978	DONRUSS (Andy)	each	1-3
		set of 42	set	40-60
			pack	4-6
			wrapper	1-2
			display box	8-12
PUZZLES	1978	APC Andy Gibb 11″ x 17″		25-35
	1979	APC Bee Gees 11″ x 17″		25-35
RADIO				25-35
THERMOS	1978	THERMOS w/all 3 characters		10-15
TV GUIDE	1979			5-10

Andy Gibb Doll

Metal Lunch Boxes and Thermos

Andy Gibb Puzzle

Phonograph

Plastic Lunch Box and Thermos

Puzzles

PAT BOONE

Next to Elvis Presley no one had as much success in music in the 1950s as Pat Boone. The tamer alternative to Elvis, Pat had nearly as much success with the (other) audience. Born Charles Boone in 1934, Pat had a massive barrage of hits from 1955 to 1962. He landed a total of 38 top 40 hits, six of which became Number One. Unlike other idols Pat kept a cleaner, fresher image than many musical acts of the times. With this approach, Pat gained popularity among not only a more mellow audience of kids but their happy parents as well.

With his increasing success Pat landed a show on ABC-TV in Oct. 1957 that was sponsored by Chevrolet and ran through June of 1959. Pat had strong religious convictions that remained evident throughout his career. He taught Sunday school and delivered sermons to his church congregation. Pat's strong beliefs and sense of good helped create his popular book "Twixt Twelve and Twenty" that sold more than 200,000 copies in just two months. The book offered teens some realistic looks at life, advise on situations and general moral issues that are pertinent through the teen years. This book not only sold well in the teen market but also was heralded by parents as an inspiration.

Pat Boone offered the other side of the coin to music listeners and rebel teen idols of the 1950s. His music and beliefs were well accepted by his audience. Though he failed to have a lasting music (top 40) career, he is remembered fondly through time.

Like other teen idols, Pat Boone had a fair amount of memorabilia created through the years. Though Pat's memorabilia has all but disappeared, what items survived are considered scarce and valuable. Unlike many others, even Pat's paper items are considered of value. Not many toy items were created since, for the most part, his audience was that of the over 12 market. Pat Boone items in any above Grade 7 condition are of worthy investment.

BEACH TOWEL	1958	38″ X 20″	100-125
CHARM BRACELET	1958	COOGA MOOGA INC. carded	75-125
JEWEL BOX	1958	COOGA MOOGA INC.	100-150
LAMP	1958	wall type has picture and song titles	200-300
LIFE MAGAZINE	1959	FEB. cover	5-8
NECKLACE	1958	COOGA MOOGA INC. carded	75-125
NYLONS	1958	COOGA MOOGA INC. packaged	95-115
PAPERDOLLS	1959	WHITMAN	40-75
PARTY CUPS		set of 4 in box	40-60
PHONOGRAPH	1958	COOGA MOOGA INC.	NPA
RADIO	1958	COOGA MOOGA INC.	NPA
RECORD TOTE	1958	COOGA MOOGA INC. vinyl	100-175
SOCKS	1958	COOGA MOOGA INC. w/band	40-70
SUNGLASSES	1958	COOGA MOOGA INC.	75-125
WALLET	1958	COOGA MOOGA INC. vinyl	100-200
WATCH	1958	COOGA MOOGA INC.	NPA
WRITING TABLET	1958		15-25

It is believed that most of the above items were created by Pat Boone's Company Cooga Mooga Inc.

Paper Dolls

Life Magazine

CALIFORNIA RAISINS

It's hard to say what the late Marvin Gaye would think of a bunch of raisins singing his number one song some 20 years later. But with the success of a very well executed advertising campaign, the California Raisins became extremely popular. Not only did the fruit benefit from this publicity but the toy market as well.

In 1987 with the establishing of the raisins came a huge wave of merchandise to follow. At first the merchandise related to the product it was created for. But, by 1988 most every item imaginable was being produced. From lunch boxes to wind socks, even small figures resembling famous music stars and shaped like raisins were seen. The caliber of their success was that equal to a highly successful rock band. And the merchandise produced was as great or greater.

Like the Banana Splits, the Raisins never produced a top 40 release, but did relate to rock and roll through their ties with music. Like the Splits their popularity was strong with kids. They, too, were good clean fun, harmless and collectible.

The California Raisins' merchandise is popular today and will be in the future by several different types of collectors. With the increasing popularity of advertising figure collectors, the Raisins merchandise is already popular. Rock and roll and toy collectors are scurrying to absorb any merchandise of the Raisins they too can find. And, nostalgia collectors are picking up Raisin items for their collectible zeal. Many unusual items were produced and marketed. Many of these items are of value through the collectors' channels already and with their broad appeal are sure to grow in popularity and value.

AIR FRESHENERS	1988	MEDO various figures	each 3-5
BACK PACK	1988	CAL RAB APPLAUSE 15″ vinyl	15-20
BANK	1987	vinyl	10-15
BOOKS	1988	CHECKERBOARD PRESS various titles	3-5
CARDS		HARDEES 2 1/2″ x 3 1/2″	each 2-4
	1988	stickers DIAMOND set of 180	each .15-.20
			set 35-40
			wrapper .15-.20
			sticker album 4-8
CARD GAME	1987	DECIPHER INC.	5-8
CHALKBOARD	1988	ROSE ART 12″ x 16″	10-12
CLAY FACTORY	1988	ROSE ART	30-40
COLORFORMS	1987	COLORFORMS	15-20
COLORING BOOK	1988	MARVEL	5-10
CROSS STITCH PATTERNS	1988	CAL RAB	each 3-5
CRAYON BY NUMBER	1988	ROSE ART	30-40

FIGURES

CALRAB Various figures

Lead singer, eyes closed, w/microphone	3-4
Conga Dancer w/blue tennis shoes and raised left hand	3-4
Conga dancer w/orange tennis shoes and sunglasses	3-4
Saxophone playe	3-4
Orange tennis shoes and sunglasses w/blue (horizontal) surfboard	7-8
Orange tennis shoes and sunglasses w/blue (vertical) surfboard	7-8
Guitar player w/red guitar and blue shoes	5-6
Lady dancer w/hot pink heels	4-5
Blue glasses w/blue tennis shoes	5-6
Guy winking with pink tennis shoes	5-6
Candy cane raisin	4-5
Santa raisin	4-5
Bass Player	6-7
Drummer	9-10
Lady w/lowered tambourine and green heels	4-5
Lady w/raised tambourine and yellow heels	4-5
Lady valentine "Be Mine" w/pink heels	4-5
Valentine "I'm yours" w/red tennis shoes	4-5

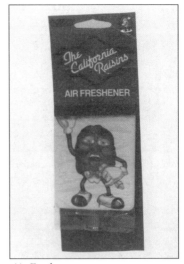
Air Freshener

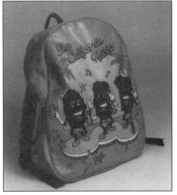
Backpack

Chalkboard

Clay Factory

Cross Stitch Patterns

Coloring Book

Conga Dancer with Blue Shoes/Lead Singer/Conga Dancer with Sunglasses/Sax Player

Girl with Raised Tambourine/Girl with Hot Pink Heels/Girl with Lowered Tambourine

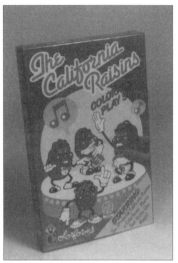

Colorforms

Crayon By Number

FIGURES, cont.

Boy singer, eyes open, w/microphone and outstretched left arm	5-6
Girl singer w/yellow heels and microphone	5-6
Hip guitar player w/yellow guitar and headband	12-15
Sax player w/beret	5-6
Male w/orange sunglasses, sitting in beach chair	4-5
Sandals and green trunks w/surfboard	4-5
Girl with grass hula skirt	4-5
Girl sitting on sand w/green shoes	4-5
Piano player "Red"	15-20
"AC" w/ red shoes and left hand extended in "low five" postion	30-35
"Mom" Lulu Arborman	30-35
Michael Raisin	20-25
The Graduate (w/microphone)	15-20
The Graduate (Conga dancer w/blue shoes)	15-20
The Graduate (Conga dancer w/orange sunglasses)	15-20
The Graduate (w/saxophone)	15-20

HARDEE'S RAISINS Figures

Lead singer w/microphone	1-2
Conga dancer w/blue tennis shoes and both hands raised	1-2
Conga dancer w/orange tennis shoes and sunglasses	1-2
Saxophone player	1-2
Guitar player w/blue guitar and orange tennis shoes	1-2
Trumpet player	1-2
Roller skater	1-2
Skateboard	1-2
Yellow tennis shoes and sunglasses with boom box	1-2

Christmas Raisins

AC Red Shoes/Piano Player/Drummer

Michael Raisin

Valentine Raisins

Hip Guitar Player/Girl Singer/Boy Singer/Sax Player

Girl with Grass Hula Skirt/Girl sitting on Sand/Male with Orange Glasses/Male with Sandals/Green Trunks and Surfboard

FIGURES, cont.

Red tennis shoes and sunglasses with yellow surfboard		
"Anita Break" w/shopping bags and violet heels	4-5	
"Allota Style" w/boom box and pink boots	4-5	
"Buster" with black and yellow tennis shoes and skateboard	4-5	
"Benny" with bowling ball and bag	4-5	

"BENDEE" RAISINS

Lead singer, eyes closed, w/microphone	8-10
Conga dancer w/blue tennis shoes	6-8
Conga dancer w/orange tennis shoes and sunglasses	6-8

CLAYMATION FRIENDS

Rudy Bagaman	4-5
Lick Broccoli	4-5
Banana White	4-5
Cecil Thyme	15-20
Leonard Limabean	15-20
(figure list courtesy of Larry De Angelo)	

Finger Puppet

FINGER PUPPET	1987	CALRAB 8″ Foam rubber	5-8
GAME	1987	CLARAB Decipher Inc	15-20
GLASS	1987	CALRAB 5 1/2″	5-8
HALLOWEEN COSTUME			10-15
JIGSAW PUZZLE	1988	APC 75pcs	5-10
	1988	APC 500pcs	5-10
LAPEL PINS	1988	CALRAB 1 1/2″ metal/enamel	each 2-3
	1988	APPLAUSE 1 3/4″ figural	5-8
LUNCHBOXES	1987	THERMOS plastic	5-10
	1988	THERMOS plastic	5-8
MUGS	1987	3 1/2″ ceramic (H.B-day)	12-15
	1987	5 1/2″ plastic	3-8

Glass

Graduate Set

Claymation Friends: Cecil Thyme/Banana White/Rudy Bagaman/Lick Brocoli/Leonard Limabean

Game

Lapel Pins, Enamel Finish

Happy Birthday Mug with Box

Jigsaw Puzzle, 75 pieces

Jigsaw Puzzle, 500 pieces

Lunchboxes and Thermos

RAIN COAT		pink	10-12
STICKER ALBUM	1988	CALRAB	3-5
TARGET GAME	1988	12″ foam rubber	10-12
THERMOS	1987-88	THERMOS	2-3
WALKERS	1987	NASTA 5″ wind-ups	each 4-6
		carded	8-12
WATCHES	1988	NELSONIC singer	10-12
	1988	NELSONIC girl w/tambourine	10-12
		fan club watch	10-12
WINDSOCK	1988		15-25

Figural Lapel Pin

Plastic Mug

Sticker Album

Walker

Alvin, Theodore and Simon became popular in 1958 when their hit, "The Chipmunk Song" spent four weeks at Number One. The nostalgic christmas song was just the beginning for the Chipmunks' popularity through time. From 1958-1962 the group charted a total of eight top 40 entries, equal to such heavy hitters as the Culture Club and The Doors. Though their album sales didn't compare, their popularity did and continues to today.

Through their creator's success with a previous Number One single, "Witch Doctor" in April of 1958 Ross Bagdasarian (using the name David Seville) began experimenting with sound. By speeding up vocal tracks The Chipmunks were born. For the first time in history animals were seen playing Rock and Roll. The Chipmunks paved the way for such acts as The Banana Splits and The Bugaloos.

With the success of the songs CBS-TV aired a prime time animated series entitled "The Alvin Show" on October 14, 1961. The original show ran through September 12, 1962 for a total of 26 episodes. The show hit pay dirt with the kids. The Chipmunks have held the test of time and are certainly a part of our Americana history.

Many items have been marketed for the Chipmunks and in particular for their leader Alvin. Chipmunk toys were first produced in the late 1950s. The early Chipmunk figures were very unlike the figures we see today. The first figures created resembled that of actual chipmunks with a large letter representing their name monogrammed on their shirts. As their popularity increased the figures transformed into cuter characters, ones that children could relate better with. Another transition appeared in 1983 with the addition of other characters including the Chipettes. A final change occurred in the late 1980s when the three main characters took on a more youthful appearance.

Chipmunks' memorabilia is available, fun and collectible. Most of the early merchandise (pre 1970) is of substantial value today. The vinyl lunch kit produced in 1962 is perhaps the most highly desired of all the Chipmunks' collectibles. The challenging aspect of collecting Chipmunk memorabilia is that since so many items were produced it's nearly impossible to discover them all. Even serious Chipmunk collectors will constantly find items that they never knew existed.

Alarm Clock

Bandages

Alvin Bank

ALARM CLOCK	1990	DAYTON HUDSON	10-15
ALVIN TATTOOS	1966	FLEER 2 sizes	each 8-10
			pack 45-50
			wrapper 30-40
BANDAGES	1990	DAYTON HUDSON	2-4
BANK	1984	CBS TOYS Alvin rubber	10-12
BOOKS	1959	LITTLE GOLDEN BOOK	
		"Chipmunks Merry Xmas"	15-25
	1966	WHITMAN "The ocean blues"	25-30
		WONDER BOOK "Alvins lost voice"	20-30
BOWL	1959	3 Chipmunks pre-cartoon	40-50
CARD GAME	1963	ED-U-CARDS	15-20
COLORING BOOK	1960	SAALFIELD pre-cartoon	40-45
	1966	SAALFIELD & WHITMAN	30-35
COMICS	1962	number 1	15-20
		all others (60s)	3-10
CUP DISPENSER	1984	HELM for paper cups	15-20
CURTAIN CALL THEATER	1984	IDEAL	30-40
DOLLS	1987	BURGER KING 7″ plush set of 3	ea. 4-8
	1983	CBS 12″ plush set of 3	ea. 8-10
	1963	KNICKERBOCKER 14″ plush set of 3	ea. 40-50
	1983	IDEAL 10″ Dressable set of 3	ea. 5-15
	1983	IDEAL talking 18″ plush set of 3	ea. 25-40
DOLLS	1983	IDEAL wind-ups 4″ plastic set of 7 Uncle Harry, Eleanor, Jeanette, Brittany, Alvin, Simon and Theodore	ea. 5-12
DOLLS	1983	IDEAL paint and play figures set of 7 same figures as above	ea. 3-8
DOLLS	1983	IDEAL poseable play pals 4″ Alvin, Simon, Theodore,Brittany, Jeanette, Eleanor, Uncle Harry, Alvin (in concert), Simon (in concert), Theodore (in concert).	ea. 2-5
DOLLS	1983	IDEAL play pals 2 1/2″ set of 19 Simon the magician, Alvin the angel, Theodore the diver, Uncle Harry, Super Alvin, Brittany, Simon w/guitar, Alvin with Harmonica, Theo-	ea. 2-5

Book

Comics

Curtain Call Theater

Poseable Play Palls Dolls

Play Pals Dolls

Burger King 7" Alvin Doll

DOLLS, 1983, cont.

dore with drums, Theodore the Chef, Simon the doctor, Alvin the cowboy, Jeanette the Chipette, Brittany the Chipette, Eleanor the Chipette, Simon with baseball bat, Alvin the boxer, and Theodore the skater.

DOLLS	1983	IDEAL playpals figures 2 1/2" set of 3 (4 sets) Musican theme, Sports theme, When I grow up theme, and Alvin and Friends theme.	set 8-15
EASY SHOW MOVIES	1969	KENNER	30-40
FLASHLIGHT	1991	DEL MONTE sendaway	20-25
FOOT STOOL	1963	KNICKERBOCKER	65-75
GAMES	1960	HASBRO Acorn hunt	65-70
	1960	HASBRO Big Record	50-60
	1960	HASBRO Cross Country	60-70
	1983	IDEAL Go Hollywood	15-20
GLASSES	1990	plastic 10 oz. chimpunks	4-8
	1985	glass 12 oz. set of 4	ea. 5-8
GREETING CARDS	1964	BUZZA/CARDOZO came w/record	10-15
HAND PUPPET	1990	DAYTON HUDSON 9" plush	5-8
	1963	KNICKERBOCKER 10" cloth w/vinyl head	30-40
HALLOWEEN COSTUME	1962	Alvin	75-150
HARMONICA	1959	PLASTIC INJECT. CO. carded	75-85
INFLATABLES	1964	IDEAL	30-40
JIGSAW PUZZLE BOOK	1987	Burger King 4" x 4"	3-5
KITE	1960s	ROALEX	55-65
LOOT BOX	1959	vinyl storage box pre-cartoon	45-55
LUNCH BOXES	1963	THERMOS vinyl	300-375

Ideal 10" Alvin Doll

Talking Alvin Doll

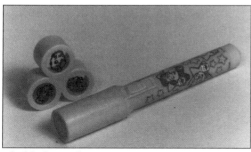

Flashlight Send-away

Wind-up figures

Glasses

Alvin Handpuppet

Jigsaw Puzzlebook

	1984	THERMOS plastic	5-10
MAGIC DRAWING SLATE	1962	SAALFIELD	30-40
MARRIONETTE	1962	KNICKERBOCKER (Alvin)	60-80
MUGS	1959	pre-cartoon	30-40
OUTFITS	1983	IDEAL fits 10″ plush doll Cowboy, Boxer, Super Chipmunk Jogger, Ball player, Santa Claus	5-8
PAINT AND CRAYON SET	1959	HASBRO pre-cartoon	65-75
PICNIC BUGGY	1984	IDEAL (chipettes)	15-25
PLATE	1959	3 Chipmunks pre-cartoon	40-50
POCKET BOOK	1959	pre-cartoon with fir	65-85
PRESS-OUT BOOK	1966	WHITMAN	35-45
PRE-CARTOON DOLLS		TIMELY TOYS Alvin lg. stuffed wind-up Alvin w/ harmonica stuffed musical wind-up ragtime cowboy Joe musical	75-85 75-85 75-85
PUZZLES	1984	APC jigsaw 125 pcs.	5-8
RADIO	1983	IDEAL WKID soft radio	20-30
RECORD PLAYER		Alvin and the Chipmunks	50-75
RECORD SENDAWAY	1963	COLGATE premium w/ mailer	45-55
SLIDE TRAY PUZZLE	1959	ROALEX (Alvin)	55-65
SLIPPERS	1990	DAYTON HUDSON (Alvin)	10-15
SOAKIES	1963	COLGATE PALMOLIVE 10″ Theodore and Simon Alvin red/yellow or white/red Alvin black on white 8 1/2″	each 15-25 15-25 15-25
SOAP DISPENSER	1984	HELM boxed loose	15-20 5-8
SONG TOTE	1959	pre-cartoon vinyl	100-150
SPOON AND FORK SET	1990	DAYTON HUDSON	5-8|
SQUEEZE TOY	1964	Alvin	30-40
STICKER FUN	1966	WHITMAN	35-45
STUFF AND LACE SET	1959	HASBRO pre-cartoon	65-75

Puzzle

Plastic Lunch Box and Thermos

Vinyl Lunch Box and Thermos

TABLECLOTH	1990	HALLMARK 54″ x 102″ sealed	8-12
TELEPHONE	1984	MED. PROD. 15″ plastic Alvin	30-40
THERMOS	1963	THERMOS metal	50-75
	1984	THERMOS plastic	3-5
TOOTHBRUSH	1984	BAGDASARIAN battery operated	20-40
TOOTHBRUSH HOLDER	1984	boxed	30-45
TOTE	1990	HALLMARK 7 1/2″ x 10″ paper	3-5
TREAT MOBILE	1984	IDEAL boxed	15-25
		loose	10-15
TUMBLER	1990	clear plastic	3-5
VAN	1983	IDEAL "On Tour" playset boxed	50-75
		loose	15-25
		Dave Seville Doll (came with van)	5-10
WALKIE TALKIE SET	1985	HELM TOY CORP. Alvin	20-30
WALLET	1959	3″ x 3 1/2″ white vinyl pre-cartoon	35-45
WATCH	1991	DEL MONTE sendaway	20-25
YO-YO	1991	DEL MONTE sendaway	20-25
XMAS STOCKING		vinyl	30-40

Alvin Telephone

Plastic Glass

Soakies

Walkie Talkie

Tablecloth and Tote

Alvin Slippers

Spoon and Fork Set

"On Tour" Van

DONNY /MARIE/OSMONDS ━━━━━━━━

She's a little bit country and he's a little bit rock and roll. Together they had the first musical/variety TV show to be hosted by a brother and sister, six top 40 singles and always a clean-cut image. Donny produced 11 top 40 singles in his own right. Five of these sold a million copies each within the short three-year period between 1971-73. All this before the Donny and Marie Show aired on January 23rd 1976.

The Osmond brothers – Alan, Wayne, Merrill, Jay and Donny – made history on their own well before Donny joined Marie in 1976 for the show. The Osmonds had 10 top 40 hits with such memorable songs as 'One Bad Apple' and 'Yo-Yo'. Donny, clearly the leader of the band produced solo albums and became a teen heartthrob. Following the same path as Michael Jackson and The Jackson Five, The Osmonds too had an animated cartoon series on ABC that began September 9, 1972 and ran through September 1, 1974.

The Osmond family members collectively, as a duo or solo acts were extremely successful. Even the youngest member, Jimmy, had a hit.

The Osmond family produced a vast array of memorabilia, much of which is scarce today. Many of these items are increasing rapidly in value due to their lack of availability. Some items such as the single Donny and Marie dolls are common. But without a box there is little value. Certainly boxed items would be the ones of choice. The Osmonds and Donny and Marie toys and memorabilia are good investments in today's market.

DONNY AND MARIE

TV Guide and Books

BOOKS	1977	GOLDEN PRESS Top secret project		5-8
	1977	WHITMAN State Fair Mystery		8-12
BRUNCH BAG	1977	ALADDIN vinyl (short hair)		70-125
	1976	ALADDIN vinyl (long hair)		70-125
BUTTONS	1976	OSBRO 3″ on card		8-12
CARRY CASE	1976	vinyl case for dolls		40-75
COLOR BOOK	1977	WHITMAN		10-15
COLORFORMS	1976	COLORFORMS dress-up set		30-50
COUNTRY AND ROCK RHYTHM SET	1976	GORDY tambourine and microphone		15-20
DOLL CLOTHES	1977	MATTEL 10″ X 13″ Silver and shine, Country Hoedown, Glimmer'o gold, Peasant sensation	boxed	12-20
DOLLS	1976	MATTEL 12″ Donny	boxed	20-30
	1976	MATTEL 12″ Marie	boxed	20-30
	1976	MATTEL 12″ Donny/Marie	set	75-100
	1976	MATTEL 30″ Marie modeling doll	boxed	70-100
DRESS PATTERNS	1976	BUTTERICK	each	5-8
FAN CLUB KIT	1976			40-60
GAME	1976	MATTEL TV show game		20-30
GUITAR	1977	purple		65-100
HALLOWEEN COSTUMES		Donny or Marie	ea.	20-30
LUNCH BOXES	1977	ALADDIN vinyl (short hair)		60-110
	1976	ALADDIN vinyl (long hair)		60-110
MAKE UP SET	1976	MATTEL Marie		15-30
NODDER	1970'S	Donny 9″		200-250
NOTEBOOK	1972	WESTAB loosleaf		20-25
PAPERDOLLS	1973	Marie		30-40
	1976	WHITMAN Donny and Marie		20-30
PUZZLE	1977	WHITMAN frametray		10-15
RADIO	1977	LJN AM Portable		50-75

Brunch Bag and Thermos/ Long Hair

Brunch Bag & Thermos/ Short Hair

Book

Coloring Book

Country and Rock Rhythm Set

Doll Clothes

Dress Patterns

Dolls

Game

Puzzle

Radio

RECORD CASES	1977	PEERLESS	small 20-30
	1977	PEERLESS	large 40-50
RECORD PLAYER	1977		30-40
STRING PUPPETS	1978	MADISON LTD Donny	30-50
	1978	MADISON LTD Marie	30-45
	1978	MADISON LTD Set w/both	70-100
THERMOSES	1976	ALADDIN long hair	15-25
	1977	ALADDIN short hair	15-25
TOOTH BRUSH		battery operated	50-75
TV GUIDES	1976		10-15
	1977		10-15
TV SHOW PLAYSET	1976	MATTEL	50-85
VAN	1970'S	LAPIN plastic	40-65
VANITY SET		Marie's	boxed 40-60

OSMONDS

DOLL	1978	MATTEL Jimmy	65-90
COLORING BOOK	1973		20-25
GUM CARDS	1973	DONRUSS	card .75-1.00
		set of 66	set 50-75
			pack 8-10
			wrapper 5-6
			display box 40-50
HALLOWEEN COSTUME	1978	Jimmy	20-25

Lunch Box and Thermos/Short Hair

Lunch Box and Thermos/Long Hair

Record Cases

String Puppet

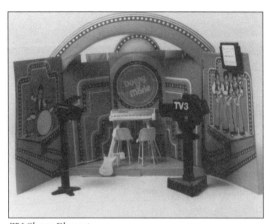
TV Show Playset

Osmonds: Lunch Box and Thermoses

LUNCH BOX	1973	ALADDIN steel	50-90
PHOTO ACTIVITY ALBUMS	1973	ARTCRAFT	15-20
STATIONERY	1973	OSBRO with jacket	40-60
THERMOS	1973	ALADDIN plastic 2 types	15-25
WALL DECORATION	1975	ROCKY MT. RAINBOW CORP.	50-60

Photo Activity Album

Osmonds: Stationery

Osmonds: Wall Decoration

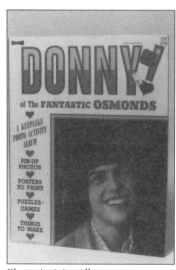
Photo Activity Album

HAMMER

With a gaining popularity of rap music in America came the need to crown a king. In perfect time came Hammertime! Hammer (born Stanley Kirk Burrell in 1962) has become the most celebrated rap music star to date. Hammer's flashy fast-paced dance routines and clever blend of past hits with bouncy rap mixes have won him super-star success in the rap circuit.

Hammer originally began as M.C. Hammer (M.C. stood for Master of Ceremonies) and through time dropped the M.C. becoming Hammer.

At a young age Hammer was a bat boy for a professional baseball team. After a time in the service and an unsuccessful attempt at col-lege, Hammer began his rap and dance routine in the Bay-area club scene. After some success Hammer convinced two old friends from his baseball years to invest in him so he could start his own record label. With this secured, Hammer recorded an album and sold the album from the trunk of his car. With the success of his album sales, came an interest from Capital records. His rise to the top came quickly.

His "Hammer, Don't Hurt E'm" album sold five million copies in a few short months. With this success came three Grammy awards and five American Music Awards. The album was the first rap album in history to create three top 10 hits on the pop charts.

Hammers ultimate clean cut success won him a short lived ani-mated cartoon series on ABC-TV in 1990. With his younger audience came a huge amount of youngster-related Hammer memorabilia. Everything was created from dolls and puzzles to a whole string of school supplies. Much of Hammer's memorabilia is still available through the collector's circuit. With his huge popularity Hammer mer-chandise is certain to appreciate in value with the generation that adored him.

Backpacks

Mattel Dolls

Bubble Gum Packs

Hammer Clothes

BACKPACK	1991	BUSTIN PROD. 15″ vinyl 2 styles		15-20
BUBBLE GUM	1991	BUSTIN PROD. 5″ x 7 1/2″ pack		3-5
	1991	BUSTIN PROD. 2″ x 3 1/2″ tin		3-5
CLOTHES	1991	MATTEL rap fashions 10x13 boxed	ea.	3-5
COLLECTOR FOLDER	1991	AMUROL 3 1/2″ x 5″ (w/gum)		5-6
DOLLS	1991	MATTEL 11 1/2″ w/cassette tape		20-30
	1991	MATTEL 11 1/2″ w/boom box		25-30
FANNY PACK	1991	BUSTIN PROD.		5-8

Jigsaw Puzzles, Small & Large

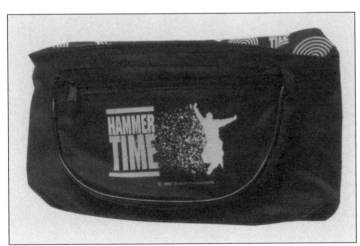

Fanny Pack

Lunch Box and Thermos

School Folders

Wallets

Patterns

JIGSAW PUZZLES	1990	MILTON BRADLEY 500 pcs.		5-8
	1991	MILTON BRADLEY 100 pcs.		3-5
LUNCH BOX	1991	THERMOS plastic		5-10
NOTE BOOK	1991	BUSTIN PROD. 3″ x 5″		3-5
	1991	BUSTIN PROD. 8″ x 10 1/2″		5-8
PATTERNS	1991	SIMPLICITY (various)	ea.	5-8
RAP MICROPHONE	1991	IMPACT TOY		20-25
SCHOOL FOLDER	1991	BUSTIN PROD. 10″ x 12″		1-3
SCHOOL KIT	1991	BUSTIN PROD. (came w/various school supplies)		8-10
SLAP BRACELET	1991	BUTTON-UP on card		5-6
THERMOS	1991	THERMOS plastic		2-5
VIDEO GAME	1991	TIGER ELECTRONICS LCD		20-25
VIEWMASTER	1991	TYCO		3-5
WALLETS	1991	BUSTIN PROD. various styles		8-12

Rap Microphone

Small Notebook & School Kit

Video Game

Viewmaster

If one word could describe Michael Jackson, it would be nothing short of "brilliant." Not one person to date has successfully mastered the music business like Michael. Learning to sing and dance at a young age was to be his key to success. With his unrelenting desire for perfection throughout his recording career, Michael has understood the chemistry needed to change with the times and reap the benefits of doing so. The unbelievable aspect of Michael is that his singing, dancing, popularity and compassion for others continues to grow.

By the time Michael was 15 years old he had attained 13 top 40 hits with his brothers as the Jackson 5 and four top 40 singles of his own. Michael's career then soared to a level no other musician has been able to match with the release of the "Thriller" album in 1984. The album sold over 40 million copies to become the best selling album of all time.

Due in part to his growing up in the business, Michael has had his share of tabloid gossip, even more it seems than the weekly sightings of the late Elvis Presley. But through it all – fame, fortune and unprecedented success, Michael is more than a mega star. His humane nature and willingness to share has helped many throughout the world with his support of and donations to humanitarian programs.

The Jackson 5's popularity in the early 1970s won them a spot on ABC as an animated cartoon series. The Saturday morning cartoon aired on September 11, 1971 and ran through September 1, 1973. The Jackson 5 also hosted several other musical variety shows on CBS in the mid 1970s.

Since not much was produced, Jackson 5 memorabilia is scarce and demands attention. Michael Jackson memorabilia is becoming valuable quickly and is still found commonly at collectors' shows. Finding memorabilia in excellent to mint condition is important since the higher graded items are still in supply at affordable prices, and are sure to increase steadily in the future due to Michaels super star success.

Belts

Card Set

Colorforms Dress-up Set

Doll Clothes

Binder/Notebook/Address Book

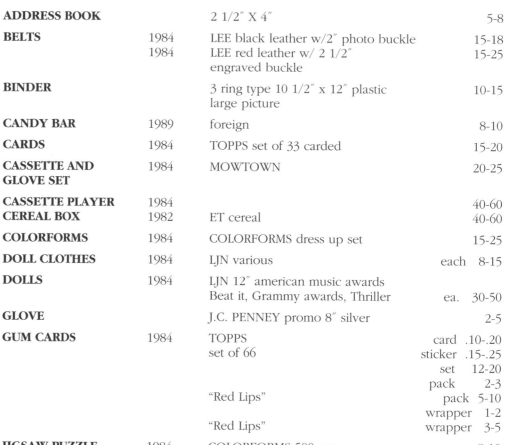

Dolls

ADDRESS BOOK		2 1/2″ X 4″	5-8
BELTS	1984	LEE black leather w/2″ photo buckle	15-18
	1984	LEE red leather w/ 2 1/2″ engraved buckle	15-25
BINDER		3 ring type 10 1/2″ x 12″ plastic large picture	10-15
CANDY BAR	1989	foreign	8-10
CARDS	1984	TOPPS set of 33 carded	15-20
CASSETTE AND GLOVE SET	1984	MOWTOWN	20-25
CASSETTE PLAYER	1984		40-60
CEREAL BOX	1982	ET cereal	40-60
COLORFORMS	1984	COLORFORMS dress up set	15-25
DOLL CLOTHES	1984	LJN various	each 8-15
DOLLS	1984	LJN 12″ american music awards Beat it, Grammy awards, Thriller	ea. 30-50
GLOVE		J.C. PENNEY promo 8″ silver	2-5
GUM CARDS	1984	TOPPS	card .10-.20
		set of 66	sticker .15-.25
			set 12-20
			pack 2-3
		"Red Lips"	pack 5-10
			wrapper 1-2
		"Red Lips"	wrapper 3-5
JIGSAW PUZZLE	1984	COLORFORMS 500 pcs	8-10
KEYCHAINS	1988	brass 1 1/2″ x 3 3/4″ concert promo	8-12
	1984	plastic 1 1/2″ x 3″ 5 cards 2 sided	3-6
	1984	brass 2 1/2″ x 3 1/4″ Thriller	3-6
	1984	plastic 1 1/2″ x2 1/4″ Thriller w/telephone log	5-8
LIFE MAGAZINE	1984	SEPT.	3-5
MICROPHONE	1984	LJN cordless electric	boxed 20-30

Jigsaw Puzzle

Mug

Paperweight

Life Magazine

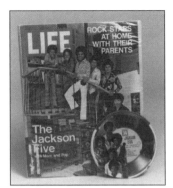

J-5 Life Magazine/Record

Cassette and Glove Set

Pets

MUG		3 1/2″ ceramic "I love" (lips) Michael Jackson	10-18
NOTEBOOK	1984	spiral	5-8
PAPER WEIGHT		Thriller 4 1/2″ x2 1/2″ clear resin	40-60
PETS	1987	IDEAL 10 different animals	boxed 20-30
PEPSI CANS	1984	Jacksons world tour	4-8
	1984	Jacksons world tour bank	4-8
PIN BACK BUTTON	1984	1 1/2″ x 2 1/4″ Thriller w/spring up flag	8-10
		All other assorted	.50-3
PUFFY STICKERS		set of 6 different per pack	3-5
RADIO	1984	ERTL	25-35
RECORD PLAYER	1984		45-75
RECORD PREMIUM		ET CEREAL	30-40
SCARF	1983	NIKRE 12″ X 23″	4-8
SCHOOL FOLDER	1983	BRIGHT IDEAS 9 3/4″ X 12″	4-6
SUPER STICKERS	1984	TOPPS	each 1.00-2.00
		set of 13 5″ x 7″	set 15-18
			wrapper .75-1.00
			display box 8-10
VIEW MASTER	1984	GAF talking	15-25
	1984	GAF thriller	4-8
	1984	GAF thriller gift set	15-25
WALLET	1984	3 1/2″ x 5″ nylon asst. colors	4-8
WATCH	1984	LED red leather strap	6-12
		cap. EO Disneyland	15-20
GAME	1972	SHINDANA J-5	65-100
GROOVIE BUTTONS	1972	APLHA BITS CEREAL set of 3 J-5	25-30
LIFE MAGAZINE	1971	SEPT. J-5 on cover	10-15
RECORD	1972	cereal box cut out	6-10
TV BOOK	1972	JOBETE MUSIC J-5	10-15

Viewmaster Gift Set and Viewmaster

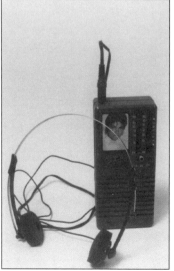

Radio

Series 1 & 2 Gum Card Wax Packs

Wallet, Super Sticker/Puffy Stickers/Pepsi Can/Watch

JOSIE AND THE PUSSYCATS———

Seven days after the Banana Splits died Josie and The Pussycats were born. After having two successful years with the Splits, Hanna-Barbera created another answer to rock and roll kid-style. The Pussycats ran from September 12, 1970 to September 2, 1972 (CBS) almost exactly the same amount of days as the Splits. Due in part to the TV success of the Beatles, Monkees and (of course) The Banana Splits, Josie was a hit.

The series began as a spin off from the Archie comic series. The Pussycats were an all-girl rock-group that was made up of Josie (group leader), Melody (dumb blonde, drummer) and Valerie (group guitarist). Casey Kaseem's voice was used as Alexander Cabot, the groups' manager. The 30-minute show ran for a total of 26 episodes and was followed up in 1972 with a spin-off series "Josie and the Pussycats in Outer Space" that ran for another two years. Josie and the Pussycats were a real-life Rock group. However, unlike the Beatles and Monkees that enjoyed musical success from their TV show, the Pussycats never cracked the top 40. Far from the usual marketing flood of items usually created for a children's Rock show, not much memorabilia was created for the Pussycats. What was issued is of value today. Cereal premium hunters and Rock collectors have been scouting Josie memorabilia for years. With few items in production and their relative scarcity most Josie items are in demand and usually hard to find in fine to mint condition. Once again, condition is extremely important with regard to value. Items that were likely to show wear with the slightest use, like the Pussycats' pencil toppers, increase substantially for each upgrade (ie. fine/good to excellent/grade 8) and are a prize to find in any (above 7) grading condition.

BOOK	1976	RAND McNALY Bag Factory Detour	5-10
COLORING BOOK			30-40
COMIC BOOKS	1971	(ARCHIE SERIES) Radio comics #1	30-40
CUP W/HANDLE	1971		10-15
GLASS	1977	16 oz.	20-25
JIGSAW PUZZLE			40-50
PAPERDOLLS	1971	WHITMAN	40-55
PATCHES		came in Wonder Bread	5-8
PENCIL TOPPERS	1969	cereal premium various	ea. 25-30
PENDANT JEWELERY	1973	LARAMI	30-40
RECORD	1972	KELLOGGS premium	15-25
SLIDE VIEWER	1972	KENNER (film strip)	15-20
SLURPEE CUP			10-15
SPOONS	1969	KELLOGS premium 4 in set assorted colors	ea. 25-30
TATTOOS		came in gum packs	ea. 5-10
WRISTWATCH	1971	BRADLEY came with 3 bands	300-350

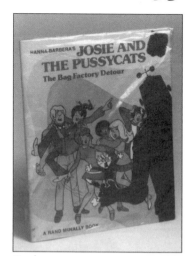

Book

Glass, Cup and Spoons

Slide Viewer

Pendant Jewelry

It's hard to believe a band with no television exposure and only one fluke top ten hit could attract so much attention. But somehow the masked members of Kiss did. It was obviously only a matter of time and the evolving transition of glitzy Glam rock of the early 1970s before someone would cover their entire face in make-up for added attention. Gene Simmons, Paul Stanley, Ace Frehley and Peter Criss took glam rock one step farther for unprecedented success. They wore outrageous costumes, presented unbelievable stage shows and wowed their fans who couldn't (or wouldn't) relate to the coexisting disco movement.

Kiss music (except curiously for their only Number 7 hit, Beth) brought back the danger element of rock music. Along with this was the mystery of who they really were. Although Kiss never made it in the pop market, the group won millions of fans in the rock and roll field. From their growing popularity in 1975 came the creation of the Kiss army (the group's fan club) which was just the beginning of what was to become one of the largest memorabilia merchandising floods of all time.

Up to this point only Elvis Presley and The Beatles had enjoyed success of this caliber from the sale of toys and memorabilia. But both of these acts had a huge listenership on AM radio and lots of exposure through television. This baffled critics. For the very first time a rock (as opposed to pop) band could support itself.

Kiss memorabilia is extremely collectible and somewhat scarce. The question is, with so many items produced, in the not too distant 70's, where did it go? Kiss items from the 1970s are becoming as hard to find as Elvis items from the 1950s and Beatles items of the 1960s though many are not as valuable. The scarcity of Kiss items will only increase their collective and investment potential in the Rock and Roll and toy markets.

Backpack

Colorforms

Combs

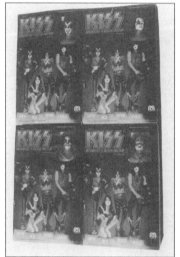

Dolls

BACKPACK	1979	Thermos	50-110
BEACH TOWEL	1978	2 Different	75-100
BED SPREAD	1978		75-135
BELT BUCKLE	1976	Brass w/ LOGO	20-35
	1977	Various picture types	25-40
CLOCK	1977	Wall type	75-150
COINS	1979	MARDI-GRAS red or silver	10-15
COLORFORMS	1979	COLORFORMS	35-60
COMBS	1980	(Foreign) various colors	each 7-10
COMICS		Number 1 Marvel	45-75
		Number 2 Marvel	40-60
CUPS	1978	Plastic 7-11 various	25-35 ea.
CURTAINS			65-100
DOLLS	1978	Mego 12″ loose	ea. 40-60
		set of 4 boxed	ea. 90-120
FAN CLUB KIT		Kiss Army	45-75
GAME	1978	AUCOIN Kiss on tour	40-75
GUITAR	1977		loose 65-100
			sealed 125-225
GUITAR PICS		assorted	each 10-12
GUM CARDS	1978	DONRUSS	card .50-.75
		set of 132	set 30-40
		consists of 2 sets	pack 3-5
			wrapper .30-.40
			display box 10-25

Note: Cards with replacement Drummer Eric Carr
(21 total) are valued at 2-3 each.

Game

Gum Card Display Boxes

Guitar

Halloween Costume

Key Chains

Lunch Box and Thermos

Makeup Kit

Pen and Pencil Set

Radio and Box

HALLOWEEN COSTUME	1978	(4) Boxed	30-60 ea.
		mask only	15-20
HAT		Firehouse (Paul Stanley)	125-250
KEYCHAINS	1977-79	Various	30-45
LUNCH BOX	1979	Thermos steel	50-85
MAKE-UP KIT	1978	Remco (2 different)	50-110 ea.
MICROPHONE			50-100
NECKLACE	1977/78	Aucoin various	25-45 ea.
NOTEBOOKS	1978/79	Various	15-25 ea.
PENCILS	1978	Set of four	sealed 45-75
			set loose 30-60
			each 10-15
PENNANTS	1977-79		15-25
PENS	1978	Set of four	carded 40-55
			set loose 50-75
			each 12-18
PILLOW			50-80
PINBALL MACHINE		working	750-1500
		not working	300-500
POSTER ART	1977		30-50
PUZZLES	1977-78	(Jigsaw) Various	35-50 ea.
RADIO	1977	boxed	75-100
		unboxed	50-75
RECORD PLAYER			175-300
			boxed 400-475
RINGS	1978	Set of four	each 15-25
			set 50-100

Puzzles

Necklaces

Trash Can

Rub n' Play

Screamer

Tour Jacket (Front)

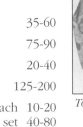

Tour Jacket (Back)

RUB N' PLAY	1979	COLORFORMS	35-60
SCREAMER	1978-79	concert promo.	75-90
SHOELACES	1977		20-40
SLEEPING BAG	1978	WASHINTON QUILT CO.	125-200
STICKERS (Puffy)	1977-78	Set of four	each 10-20 set 40-80
THERMOS	1979	Thermos plastic	10-15
TOUR JACKET	1978	concert promo.	150-175
TRASH CAN	1978		75-150
TUMBLERS	1978	2 Sets of 4	each 25-40 set 100-175
VAN (Model kit)	1977	AMT	50-85
VAN	1979	Radio controlled	100-225
VIEW MASTER	1978	GAF	sealed 40-50 opened 20-35

Model Kit

View Master

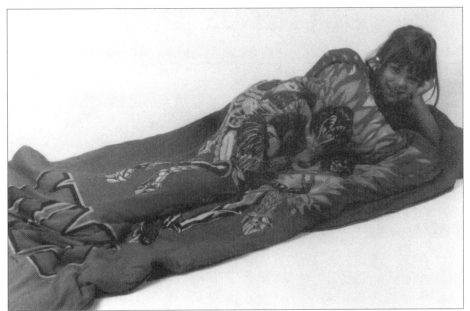

Sleeping Bag

MADONNA

It seems with Madonna you have two choices: either you love her, or hate her. Whichever you chose you can't deny her popularity and success. In addition to being number one in more countries than any singer, Madonna has also become the most successful singer on records. Madonna's strong musical and acting careers, together with her views on sexuality have made her a household name. Her unrelenting desire to succeed and being at the right place at the best time have kept Madonna always slightly ahead of the game. One always guesses what she'll do next.

Madonna did to fashion in the 1980s what Sonny and Cher did to a generation 20 years earlier. With her success came the age of the Madonna look alikes. But, Madonna always goes farther and creates so many new looks that its hard to keep up with her latest style.

While Madonna's pro-disco music was climbing the charts to make her a star, Penthouse and Playboy magazines published some nude photos taken of her years before. The successful sales of these magazines prompted a new age of Madonna, one of pushing the limits in sexuality (and a lack, some feel, of moral guidelines) to unseen heights. Madonna's success on the screen has also made her a credible actress. But it's really her character that leaves people (and it probably always will) guessing.

Madonna's book entitled "Sex" was released in 1992 to a "not so shy" audience. The book proved once again that Madonna could push the limits, achieve new heights, and, as usual, be slightly ahead of the game.

It is likely that Madonna's memorabilia will become of collectible value. Many items have been merchandised by Boy Toy Inc. (Madonna's Company) and distributed through her fan club. Though many items are currently available through the fan club, not many have made their way into the collectors' circuit. Breathless Mahoney items (from the character she played in the film "Dick Tracy") have disappeared rapidly from circulation in the relatively short time they have been available. The 18″ Breathless doll doubled in value in just a few months after its debut. This is a good indication of what the future market may hold for Madonna memorabilia.

Calendar/Book "Sex"

Fan Club Kit

Comics

BACKSTAGE PASS CARDS		on necklace	8-12
BEACH TOWELS		30˝ x 60˝ True Blue, Erotica, Bad Girl	30-35
BOOK	1992	WARNER BROS. "Sex"	loose 20-25
		in mylar cover	50-55
BUTTON PACK	1992	2˝ size set of 6	8-10
CALENDERS		ROCK EXPRESS 12˝ x 17˝	10-12
CANTEEN	1990	SELANDRA 16 oz. (Breathless)	8-12
CLUB CARD	1990	gold diggers club (Breathless)	5-8
COMICS	1990-91	REVOLUTIONARY	3-5
DOLLS	1990	PLAYMATES 18˝ Breathless	25-40
	1990	APPLAUSE 14˝ Breathless	20-25
	1990	APPLAUSE 9˝ Breathless	10-15
	1990	APPLAUSE 3 1/2˝ Breathless	3-5
EARRINGS	1992	"Play it by ear" carded	5-8
EMBLEM		2 1/2˝ X 3 1/2˝ iron on carded	5-8
FAN CLUB KIT	1993	Includes: 2-8˝ x 10˝ photos, membership card, newsletter, product catalog, folder	20-25
FANNY PACK	1990	RGA Breathless	10-15
FLYING DISC	1990	"FLIPPY FLYER" JR Nook (breathless)	8-10
JACKET	1990	Blonde Ambition Tour	150-175
JIGSAW PUZZLE	1990	MILTON BRADLEY 500 pcs	8-10
KEY CHAINS		small plastic various	3-5
LAMP	1992	17˝ Truth or Dare	40-50
LAPEL PIN	1991	1˝ metal Immaculate Logo	3-5
LIGHTER		Metal case (not licensed)	8-10

Sports Bottle/Tumbler/Canteen

Dolls

Wallet/Stickers/Patch/ Backstage Pass

Flying Disc/Fanny Pack

Lamp

Jigsaw Puzzle

Pillow

Magazines

Poster Books

Tote, Large and Small

Trash Can

MAGAZINES	1985 sept.	PENTHOUSE (nude photos)	10-15
	1985 sept.	PLAYBOY (nude photos)	15-18
MIRROR		6″ Like a Virgin	3-5
MUG	1990	plastic (Breathless)	3-5
NECKLACES	1991	Immaculate or Vogue-heart shape	5-10
PATCHES	1991	various sizes	5-8
PILLOWS	1990	13″ X 13″ Breathless	15-20
	1990	24″ X 24″ Vouge	30-35
PLAQUE	1991	14″ X 17″ Truth or Dare 2 styles	15-20
POSTER BOOKS	1986-1990		15-20
POSTCARDS		4″ X 6″ cards	set of 12 8-10
		8″ X 8″ cards	set of 5 5-8
		8″ X 10″ cards	set of 6 10-15
POSTCARD FOLDER PACK		11″ X 14″	set of 6 10-15
SPORTS BOTTLE	1990	Express yourself	3-5
STICKERS		6″ X 6″ erotica (window/perm.)	3-5
		4″ X 6″ various (foreign)	3-5
		2″ X 4″ various (foreign)	2-4
TOTE	1990	APPLAUSE 4 1/2″ X 5″ paper	3-5
		Breathless 8 1/2″ X 10″ paper Breathless	5-8
TRASHCAN	1991	18″ Truth or Dare	15-20
TUMBLER	1990	7 oz. plastic (Breathless)	8-10
WALLET	1990	black nylon 2 diff.	10-12
		Breathless	6-10
WALL HANGING	1989	45″ X 48″ Desperately seeking Susan	15-20
	1991	30″ X 45″ Vogue	10-15
WATCHES	1990	NELSONIC LED	carded 10-15
		TIMEX quartz (Breathless)	50-75
		Quartz Plastic neon 3 styles	30-35
		Quartz metal 2 styles	50-60

Watches   *Key Chains, Lapel Pin, Necklace*

After more than 400 people were interviewed, America's answer to The Beatles was born. These whimsical, nutty mop-tops became an overnight success when their show aired on NBC-TV September 12, 1966. Of the four, Mike Nesmith and Peter Tork had some musical experience. Micky Dolenz had acting experience (Circus Boy) and Davy Jones was a jockey in England who also sang in "Oliver!"

Producers Bert Schneider and Bob Rafelson created the Monkees show while Don Kirshner (with some help from his already successful songwriting friends) created massive hits for them to make famous. The zany, quick moving, prime-time TV show was based on the same format as The Beatles "Hard Day's Night" and "HELP." Their slapstick humor and two songs per show brought both the Monkees and their music instant stardom. The show ran for 58 episodes until its ratings were hurt by "Gunsmoke" and dropped in 1968.

The Monkees had a total of 11 top 40 hits, six of which went gold. But studio session musicians played the music and with the exception of some vocals, were not the Monkees at all. After gaining confidence and popularity, the Monkees severed their relationship with Kirshner, recorded a bit on their own and eventually broke up in 1970. Kirshner tried again and hit it big with the Archies. Several attempts at regrouping were tried with only marginal success with a minor hit "That Was Then, This Is Now" in 1986. The Monkees also played an important role as a stepping stone for the development of MTV (music television).

An abundance of items was created for the Monkees. With few exceptions, all Monkees memorabilia is of value. Appearing less frequently through the years, these items continue to increase in value. At recent auctions these items have demanded top dollar. Monkee items today are appreciating nearly as fast as Beatles and Kiss items.

Books

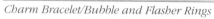

Charm Bracelet/Bubble and Flasher Rings

Finger Puppet Set

Finger Puppets

Flip Movies

Halloween Costume

BADGES	1967	DONRUSS	each	5-8
		set of 44	set	200-250
			pack	20-25
			wrapper	15-20
			display box	65-85
BOOKS	1967	WHITMAN "Who's got the Button"		15-20
		assorted paperbacks		5-10
CLOTHES TAG	1967	(photo) 5″ x 6″ Monkee fashions		25-30
CHARM BRACLETS	1967	RAYBERT various styles		25-35
COINS		plastic cereal premium		
		set of 12		100-125
COMICS	1967-68	DELL number 1		30-35
		photo covers		10-12
		all others		8-10
DOLLS	1967	HASBRO 4″ rubber show biz babies	loose ea.	25-30
			packaged	90-110
FAN CLUB KIT	1967	Included: pictures, biographies		
		badge, membership card, Newsletter		
		In original mailer		150-200
FINGER PUPPETS	1969	REMCO no Peter made	ea.	25-35
		set of 3		85-100
		sealed set of 2		100-125
GLASSES	1967	granny type		50-60
GAME	1967	TRANSOGRAM		75-125
FLIP MOVIES	1967	TOPPS	each	10-12
		set of 16	set	110-150
			pack	20-25
			wrapper	10-15
			display box	50-75
GUITARS	1966	MATTEL 14″	small	100-175
	1966	MATTEL 20″	large	135-225
GUM CARDS	1966	DONRUSS	card	1-2
			set	65-85
			pack	20-25
			wrapper	10-15
			display box	50-75

Doll Show Biz Babies, Davy   *Doll Show Biz Babies, Micky*   *Doll Show Biz Babies, Mike*

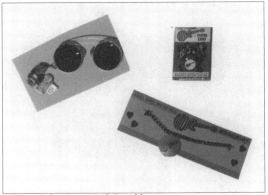
Glasses/Playing Cards/Necklace

Gum Cards

Comics

1967	series B		card	1-2
	set of 44		set	85-105
			pack	25-30
			wrapper	20-25
			display box	50-75
1967	series C		card	1-2
	set of 44		set	65-85
	"More of the Monkees"		pack	20-25
			wrapper	8-10
			display box	25-40
HALLOWEEN COSTUMES	1967	BLAND CHARNAS INC.	each	125-200
HANGER	1967	black and white cardboard		45-65
LUNCH BOX	1967	THERMOS vinyl		200-375
	1967	RAYBERT (foreign) plastic		125-200
MONKEEMOBILES	1967-68	APC 12″ tin		300-500
		CORGI 6″ (large)		175-350
		CORGI (small)		75-140
		REMCO (small)		75-140
		HUSKY (small)		75-140
MODEL KIT	1967	MPC monkeemobile		150-295
		box only		45-75
MUG	1967	ceramic		50-75
NECKLACE	1967	RAYBERT guitar logo		30-55
OIL PAINT SET	1967	ART AWARD CO. "monkeemania"		125-175
PAJAMAS	1967			135-180
PEN	1967	RAYBERT 5 1/2″ plastic		5-12
PENCIL BY NUMBER	1967			125-200

14″ Windup Guitar

Plastic Lunch Box and Thermos

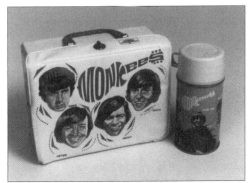
Vinyl Lunch Box and Thermos

20″ Guitar

Record/Corgi Mini Monkee Mobile

APC Tin Monkee Mobile

Corgi Monkee Mobiles, Large and Small

Talking Hand Puppet

Tambourine

PENCIL SHARPENER	1967	plastic various colors	5-10
PLAYING CARDS	1967	RAYBERT	50-75
PUNCHOUT BOOK	1967	large	75-100
PUZZLES	1967	FAIRCHILD jigsaw	30-45
RECORDS	1967-68	POST cereal box cutouts	each 5-10
RECORD CARRYING CASE	1966	MATTEL for 45 rpms	75-125
RINGS		flasher type plastic bubble type metal adj.	each 10-15 set 30-45
SHIRT	1967	brown Monkee shirt w/ logo label	125-150
TALKING HAND PUPPET	1966	MATTEL	boxed 100-150 working loose 80-100 not working loose 50-65
TAMBOURINE	1967	RAYBERT 8 1/2″	125-200
THERMOS	1967	THERMOS metal	40-65
THREE RING BINDER	1967	THERMOS	75-125
TV GUIDES	1967 1967	Jan. Sept.	25-35 20-30
VIEWMASTER	1967	GAF	40-55

Monkee Mobile Model Kit

Jigsaw Puzzle

NEW KIDS ON THE BLOCK

Not since The Beatles had any group been able to create the same emotional euphoria with fans. For nearly 20 years, countless teen idols, gimmicks and styles tried but none could match.

Then came the New Kids on the Block. Sure, they didn't write songs or play instruments like the Fab Four but a young '80s generation didn't care.

By the powers of the group's creator, Maurice Starr, (ex New Edition), Danny, Donny, Joe, Jordan, and Jonathan (brothers) were transformed into superstars. The members were recruited by Starr's talent scout and spent four years developing their act.

In the summer of 1988 the Kids (none over age 20) toured with teen-queen Tiffany and instantly became successful. All members became idols through the teeny-bop circuit. Primarily a rap music act, The Kids wowed their fans with their polished singing and dancing abilities. Much of their success was due in part to the incorporation of dance into pop music and the popularity of rap music. The New Kids, like other successful acts before them also had an animated cartoon show on saturday mornings. In light of their popularity with their young pop audience, the New Kids marketed everything.

A huge flood of items was created, marketed and sold. Their total merchandise sales was in the neighborhood of 400 million dollars in 1990 alone. Some of the items produced are still available in stores today if one is lucky enough to find them. Due to The Band's incredible popularity these items are worthy of investment for the future collectors of music memorabilia. Many items merchandised disappeared almost as fast as they were produced. Some items like the New Kids suspenders, shoelaces and keychain viewer are certain to become rare and of higher value due to their unusual nature and market scarcity.

Backpack

Binders

Blanket

BACK PACK	1990	BIG STEP PROD. 12x15	5-10
BALLOONS	1990	UNIQUE in pack	2-4
BINDER	1989	IMAGININGS 10x12 plastic	3-5
BIRTHDAY THANK-YOUS	1990	UNIQUE 8 cards sealed	2-4
BLANKET	1990	BIBB CO. 72x70	10-12
BOOK COVERS	1990	GOLDEN booklet of 8	3-5
BUBBLE GUM	1990	TOPPS set of 24	each .50-1.00
CASSETTES		full box	10-12
		box only	3-5
BUTTON PACK	1989	BIG STEP PROD. set of 6	carded 3-5
CARDS/STICKERS	1990	TOPPS	card .5-.10
		set of 176	sticker .10-.15
		consists of 2 sets	set 10-15
			wrapper .15-.20
			display box 4-8
CARD GAME	1990	MILTON BRADLEY carded	3-5
CASSETTE PLAYER	1990	BIG STEP PROD. boxed	15-20
COLORING BOOK	1990	GOLDEN	3-5
COLORFORMS	1991	COLORFORMS	10-15
COMICS	1989-90	HARVEY ROCK COMICS	each 1-2
DOLLS	1990	HASBRO 5" poseable set of 5	ea. 5-8
	1990	HASBRO 12" hagin loose set set of 5	ea. 10-15
	1990	HASBRO 12" in concert set set of 5	ea. 15-20
	1990	HASBRO 18" showtime kids,cloth set of 5	ea. 15-20
FANNY PACK	1990	WINTERLAND PROD.	5-8

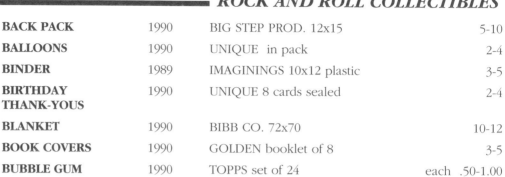

Fanny Pack

Bubble Gum Cassettes

Card Game/Board Game

Fashion Plates

Poseable Dolls

Showtime Kids

FASHION PLATES	1990	HASBRO	10-15
GAME	1990	MILTON BRADLEY	sealed 5-8
GIFT WRAP SET	1990	BIG STEP PROD.	sealed 4-6
GUM MACHINE STICKERS	1990	various sizes	each 1-2
HAT	1990	BIG STEP PROD. painters type	1-2
JIGSAW PUZZLES	1990	MILTON BRADLEY 100 pcs.	3-5
	1990	MILTON BRADLEY 500 pcs.	5-8
KEYCHAIN	1990	ROCK EXPRESS brass	sealed 5-8
		3" orange nylon backpack w/zipper	5-8
KEYCHAIN VIEWER	1990	ROCK EXPRESS assorted colors	8-10
LAPEL PINS	1990	BIG STEP PROD. carded	3-8
LOCKER MIRROR	1989	BUTTON UP 4"x6" carded	3-5
LUNCH BOXES	1990	THERMOS plastic	5-8
	1991	THERMOS cartoon plastic	5-8
MICROPHONE	1990	BIG STEP PROD.	boxed 15-20
MUGS	1989	BIG STEP PROD. 6 1/2 asst. colors	3-5
		5" plastic w/ handle asst. colors	3-5
MYLAR BALLOONS	1990	one of each character inflated	sealed 3-5
NOTEBOOK	1991	ROCK EXPRESS 3"X5"	2-5
PARTY PAC	1990	BIG STEP PROD. includes: cups plates, napkins and table cloth	5-10
PILLOW	1989	NIKRY	5-8
POSTER BOOK	1990	KIDS BOOKS INC.	3-5
RADIO	1990	BIG STEP PROD. (AM/FM) boxed	15-20
RAD ROLLERS	1990	SPECTRA STAR marbles	carded 4-6

Cards Wax Pack

Jigsaw Puzzle, 100 Pieces

Sports Bottle/Mugs

Button Pack/Key Chain/Key Chain Viewer/Locker Mirror

Small Jigsaw Puzzles

Yo-Yo

Hangin' Loose Dolls

In Concert Dolls

Socks/Slippers/Shoelaces

Stage Set

SCHOOL KIT	1990	BIG STEP PROD. includes: pencil pouch, ruler, eraser, pencil sharpener	5-8
SHOELACES	1990	BIG STEP PROD. hagin' tough	3-5
SLEEPING BAG	1990	BIG STEP PROD.	15-20
SLIPPERS	1990	GOLDBERG	pair 8-12
SOCKS	1990	BIG STEP PROD.	5-8
SPORTS BOTTLES	1989	BIG STEP PROD. 12″ var. colors	2-5
STAGE SET	1990	HASBRO	boxed 15-20
STICKERS	1990	BUTTON UP	carded 3-5
SUSPENDERS	1990	LEE	10-12
THANK-YOU CARDS	1990	BIG STEP PROD.	3-5
TELEPHONE	1990	BIG STEP PROD.	boxed 15-18
THERMOS	1990	THERMOS plastic	1-2
WATCHES	1990	NELSONIC on card	10-12
	1990	NELSONIC mix and match 5 bands	15-18
YO-YO	1990	SPECTRA STAR on card	5-8

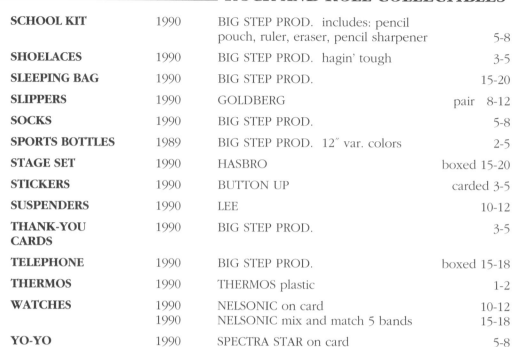

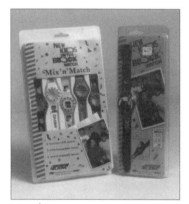
Watches

Large Jigsaw Puzzles

Lunch Boxes and Thermos

Gift Wrap Set/Party Pak/Thank You Cards/Balloons

School Kit/Suspenders/Stickers/Rad Rollers/Hat/Glasses

Radio/Telephone/Microphone/ Tape Player

After the success of the Monkees, television shows began playing an important part in rock and roll. In September 1970 on ABC-TV *The Partridge Family* took flight. The original idea was that the family's 10-year-old son, Danny, recorded a song and organized the family into a music act. The family would perform on the show and tour in their psychedelic bus promoting their records. The show did more than create ratings, it boosted two singing stars.

Shirley Jones was already a seasoned actress starring in such movies as "Carousel" and "Oklahoma", then winning an Oscar for her role in "Elmer Gantry". She also won the role of Miss Pittsburgh in 1952. With acting and singing behind her Shirley was a perfect model for the Partridge Family.

David Cassidy also had acting success before his role as Keith Partridge. He had connections with TV's Ironsides, Mod Squad, Adam-12 and several other hit shows. With his popularity rising through exposure on TV and teen magazines, David became a teen idol. When David auditioned for his role in the show it wasn't known that Shirley Jones (already selected) was his real-life step-mother, but it didn't matter. When the show aired David's first hit "I Think I Love You" was working its way up the charts as the group's first single spending three weeks at Number One. David's and Shirley's singing abilities won them a total of seven top 40 hits in just over two years. The show also starred Dave Madden (Laugh-in fame), Danny Bonaduce (played in Mayberry R.F.D, Bewitched and others) and Susan Dey, a model who had also appeared in TV commercials. The show was a success and ran through September 7, 1974 producing a total of 96 shows. The show was then followed by Partridge Family 2200 AD and was an animated cartoon series that bombed after 16 shows. David's solo success also won him four additional singles during 1971-72.

Partridge Family toys and memorabilia have a certain nostalgic charm besides their collectible value. Since the show did give way to a successful recording act (David and Shirley) the merchandise is considered Rock and Roll memorabilia and is somewhat difficult to find. The Partridge Family merchandised a wide selection of items. Their popularity among an under 12-year-old audience yielded books, dolls, gum cards and many other pre-teen items. The value of these items continues to increase steadily as the generation that embraced them becomes interested in toys and the collectible market.

Books

Books: Number 17/Young Mr. Cassidy

Bulletin Board/Magazine

Bus

BEACH TOWEL		David Cassidy	30-45
BUS	1973	REMCO plastic 14″	150-200
BOOK COVER	1971	Album insert "Up To Date"	10-15
BOOKS	1970-73	CURTIS numbers 1-16	5-10
		number 17	15-20
		"Young Mr. Cassidy"	15-20
BRACELET		charm type autographed David	50-75
BULLETIN BOARD		logo 18″ x 24″	35-45
BUTTON SET		"Partridge Family Tree"	set 50-65
		TIME SETTERS	each 15-20
CLOCK	1972	David Cassidy (wall type)	75-100
COLORFORMS	1972	David Cassidy	35-50
COLORING BOOK	1970	ART CRAFT	15-25
COMICS	1971-73	Partridges number one	15-18
		all others	5-8
	1971-73	David Cassidy	each 5-8
DOLLS	1973	REMCO Laurie Partridge 20″	100-150
	1971	IDEAL Patty Partridge 16″	125-175
FAN CLUB KIT	1971	kit included: Record, Book, mini-poster, portraits, stickers, wallet size photos, membership card, message decoder	65-95
GAME	1972	MILTON BRADLEY	10-20
GUITAR		David Cassidy 20″ plastic	50-75
GUM CARDS	1971	TOPPS	card 1.50-2.00
		series 1 set of 55	set 70-80
			pack 10-15

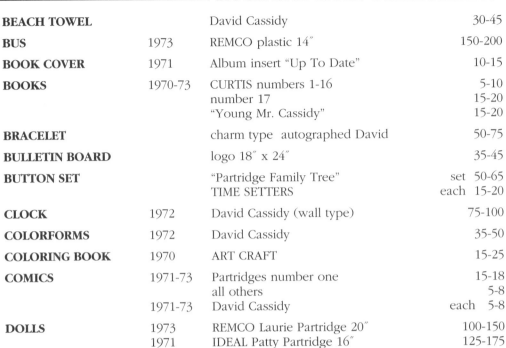

Book Cover

David Cassidy Colorforms

Partridge Family Comics

David Cassidy Comics

GUM CARDS, cont.

Laurie Partridge Doll

	series 2 set of 55	yellow wrapper 5-7	
		display box 50-85	
		card 1.00-1.50	
		set 60-70	
		pack 10-15	
		blue wrapper 5-7	
		display box 50-85	
	series 3 set of 88	card 1.50-2.00	
		set 80-100	
		pack 15-20	
		green wrapper 5-7	
		display box 30-40	

LIFE MAGAZINE	1971	(Oct.) David on cover	10-15
LUNCHBOX	1971	THERMOS steel	50-75
LUV BEADS	1971	David's choker Luv beads (sendaway)	50-75
PAPERDOLLS	1971-72	SAALFIELD Boxed Sets yellow, red or green covers	40-50
	1972	SAALFIELD "Susan Dey as Laurie"	40-50
	1971-72	ARTCRAFT "Susan Dey as Laurie"	30-40
	1972	David Cassidy paint and color album	30-40
	1973	Pictorial Activity Album	30-40
	1971-72	"The Partridge Family" red or blue cover	30-40
POSTERS	1971	TOPPS	each 8-10
		set of 24	set 160-180
			pack 20-25
			wrapper 15-20
			display box 45-60
PUZZLE	1972	APC jigsaw David Cassidy	35-45
RECORD CABINET		AMERICAN TOY 25″ x 22″ wood boxed	200-250
		no box	175-200
SHOPPING BAG		Album insert "Shopping Bag"	8-10
STICKERS	1971	David's LUV stickers (sendaway)	40-60

Guitar

Fan Club Packet

Game

Life Magazine

TV Guides

View Masters

Susan Dey Paper Dolls

THERMOS	1971	THERMOS steel	25-40
		plastic	20-30
TV GUIDES	1970	family on cover	20-30
	1971	David on cover	15-25
	1971	family on cover	15-25
	1972	David on cover	15-25
	1972	family on cover	15-25
VIEWMASTERS	1971	talking	25-30
	1971	money manager (title)	20-25
	1973	the male chauvinist	20-25
		money manager (untitled)	25-35

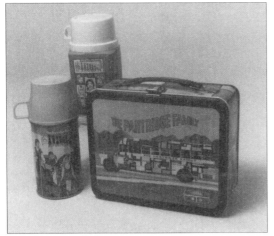

Lunch Box and Thermoses

Paper Dolls

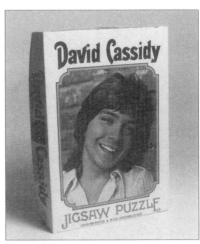

Jigsaw Puzzle

There can be no doubt in anyone's mind that without Elvis Presley, rock and roll wouldn't have been the same, or for all practical purpose may not have been at all. Elvis' efforts molded, inspired and developed Rock and Roll through the generations to what it is today. Unlike any before him Elvis had a raw and unseen talent. A talent that will quite likely never be matched again in rock history. Elvis' success in music and film won him the title "The King of Rock and Roll." He is the most popular recording artist in the history of Rock music.

When we think of Elvis, it's hard to believe he was ever anything but successful. However, in his earlier years he once drove a delivery truck for $35.00 per week. After recording several unsuccessful songs on the Sun label, Elvis' contract was sold to RCA in 1955 for an unheard of $35,000.00. His popularity quickly skyrocketed with his first hit "Heartbreak Hotel" that spent eight weeks at number one in 1956. Through his career Elvis charted an unbelievable 107 top 40 hits, more than twice that of The Beatles. He also had the most top 10 recordings and has spent more weeks in the number one position (80 weeks) than anyone else.

Elvis, like Marilyn Monroe, Jim Morrison and other famous personalities has had continuing success long after his death, possibly more than anyone in modern history. Elvis memorabilia was again fueled by his death in 1977 and continues to be made today.

With his instant success in the 1950s came the immediate need for merchandise. Elvis Presley Enterprises created a huge wave of memorabilia for hungry Elvis fans. The merchandise created by Elvis Presley Enterprises in 1956 is the most valuable and sought after of all the merchandise marketed. After his death came yet another wave of Elvis memorabilia. This merchandise is of appreciative value as well, due to his unaging interest. However, the pre 1970s merchandise continues to hold the most collectible and monetary value. The availability of most Elvis items is scarce. Especially hard to find are those items of the 1950's that have become extremely rare and continue to demand the highest of values at auctions and sales. Elvis memorabilia will always be of collectible value and is always worthy of investment.

Eugene Doll

Frame Portrait

Board Game

ASHTRAY	1956	ELVIS PRESLEY ENT.	150-275
AUTOGRAPH BOOK	1956	ELVIS PRESLEY ENT.	350-500
BELT	1956	ELVIS PRESLEY ENT. (plastic or leather)	200-300
BRACELETS	1956	ELVIS PRESLEY ENT. charm type	150-275
	1950s	ELVIS PRESLEY ENT. dog tag	100-150
	1960s	ELVIS PRESLEY ENT. (various)	100-150
BRUSH	1970s	Guitar shape	40-50
CHEW BOPS	1981	Bubble gum record (various)	ea. 3-8
COIN	1970'S	Commerative	10-15
COLORING BOOK	1984		20-30
DIARY	1956	ELVIS PRESLEY ENT.	350-500
DOLLS	1984	EUGENE 12″ various	boxed 50-100
	1987	GRACELAND 17 1/2″ w/cassette player attached	200-300
	1957	ELVIS PRESLEY ENT. 18″ vinyl with clothing	1000-2000
	1984	WORLD 21″ various	boxed 150-200
FAN CLUB KIT	1956	Includes: button, membership card, letter	300-400
FRAMED PORTRAIT	1956	ELVIS PRESLEY ENT.	300-400
GAMES	1978	DUFF "Elvis Welcomes You To His World"	65-125
	1979	BOX CAR INT. "King Of Rock"	45-75
	1956	"For The Young At Heart"	800-1200
GLASS	1956	ELVIS PRESLEY ENT. 5 1/2" clear	200-300
GUITARS	1956	ELVIS PRESLEY ENT. EMENEE	boxed 900-1500 no box 800-1000 display box 250-550
	1984	LAPIN	sealed 75-100
GUM CARDS	1956	TOPPS (bubbles) set of 66	card 10-15 set 500-700 pack 75-125 wrapper 25-65 display box 250-350
		Note: wrappers marked 5 cents are worth 10-20% more	
	1959	TOPPS (hit stars)	card 10-20
	1977	MONTY set of 50	card .75-1.00 set 45-55

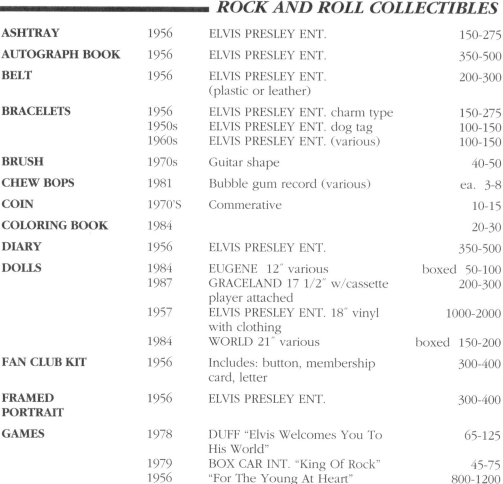

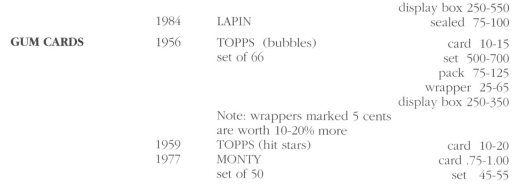

World Doll

Hat

GUM CARDS, cont.	1978	DONRUSS set of 66	card .35-.50 set 20-40 pack 3-5 wrapper 1-2 display box 8-10
	1992	RIVER GROUP set of 660 consists of 3 sets	card .20-.25 each set 20-30 pack .50-.75 wrapper .5-.10 display box 2-3
HATS	1956	ELVIS PRESLEY ENT.	65-135
HOUND DOGS	1972	Elvis summer festival 2 sizes	40-75
JIGSAW PUZZLE	1977 1992	 MILTON BRADLEY (stamp)	boxed 15-30 boxed 10-15
LIPSTICK	1956	ELVIS PRESLEY ENT. carded	700-800 loose 275-325
LIQUOR DECANTERS	1977 1977 1977 1977	15″ (1st) 15″ (2nd) 15″ (3rd) 6″ (4th)	300-400 300-400 500-600 150-200
NECKLACE	1958 1956 1962	ELVIS PRESLEY ENT. (Dog tag) ELVIS PRESLEY ENT. (love me tender) ELVIS PRESLEY ENT. (Follow that dream)	95-175 125-225 40-60
ORNAMENT	1992	HALLMARK	40-60
PAINT SET	1956	ELVIS PRESLEY ENT.	525-750
PAPERDOLL	1983	ST MARTINS PRESS	25-35
PENCILS	1956	ELVIS PRESLEY ENT. pack of 12	200-300 each 25-35

Lapin Guitar

1956 Gum Card Wrapper and Cards/1978 Gum Card Wrapper and Cards

1956 Guitar

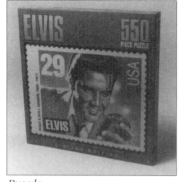

Puzzle

Ornament

Pillow, 1956

PERFUME	1957	ELVIS PRESLEY ENT. (teddy bear)	150-275
	1965	ELVIS PRESLEY ENT. (teddy bear)	50-100
PHONOGRAPH	1956	ELVIS PRESLEY ENT.	1,200-2,300
PILLOWS	1956	ELVIS PRESLEY ENT.	150-275
	1977	BOXCAR IND. (love me tender)	30-45
POCKET KNIFE	1970'S	folding type	8-15
PURSE	1956	ELVIS PRESLEY ENT. clutch type red vinyl	350-450
RADIO	1977	AM transistor type	50-75
RECORD CASE	1956	ELVIS PRESLEY ENT.	400-500
RINGS	1956	ELVIS PRESLEY ENT. (Adjustable)	50-100
	1957	Flasher ring	each 25-50
SCARF	1956	ELVIS PRESLEY ENT. (Poses and song titles)	275-400
SCRAPBOOK	1956	ELVIS PRESLEY ENT.	200-300
SIDEBURN LABEL	1956		50-75
TAPE MEASURE	1970'S		10-20
TEDDY BEARS	1957	ELVIS PRESLEY ENT.	235-350
	1971	International hotel bear	50-65
THIMBLE	1977		15-20
TIKI MUG	1961	BLUE HAWAII promo.	150-225
TRASH CAN	1977	BOX CAR IND.	65-100
TRAVEL CASE	1956	ELVIS PRESLEY ENT.	450-600
TV GUIDES	1956		50-60
	1960		30-60
WALLETS	1956	ELVIS PRESLEY ENT. w/keychain	350-450
	1956	ELVIS PRESLEY ENT (various)	300-400
WATCH	1970'S	Commerative	50-60
	1984	BRADLEY	35-50
WRAPPING PAPER	1988		50-100
VAN	1984	LAPIN plastic	70-100
WINE		"Always Elvis" white wine	30-40

Stamp

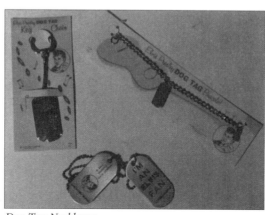

Dog Tag Necklaces

Lipstick/1957 Doll/Sideburn Label

Perfumes

Pillow, 1977

Record Case

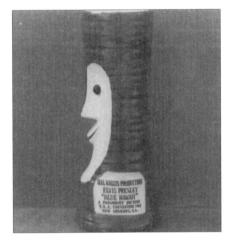

Tiki Mug

Trash Can

Clutch Purse

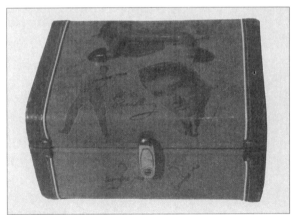

Travel Case

Hound Dogs and Teddy Bear

ROLLING STONES ────────────

According to the 1993 edition of the Guinness book of records, the Rolling Stones have every one beat when it comes to gold records. The Stones record totals are 34 gold albums, 15 platinum and 6 multi platinum. This shouldn't surprise us since the band has managed to stay together (with some additions and subtractions) longer than any other rock band (about 30 years). Their success in the early 1960's was to build them fame, and their popularity continues to be stronger than ever today.

Mick Jagger and Keith Richards first met in primary school at age 6. But it wasn't until eleven years later that they would meet again through a mutual friend. Both had interests in rhythm and blues and after spending time with other bands, formed the Rolling Stones (with Brian Jones, Ian Stewart and Dick Taylor) in 1962. The group got its name from a Muddy Waters song.

The Stones "Bad Boy" image was a perfect contrast to the Beatles who were hogging the limelight of the times. So bad was their image that they had a hard time getting national attention. Ed Sullivan didn't allow them on his show originally because he didn't like their image and didn't want to offend his viewers. It seemed where ever they played riots ensued.

Ironically, the same image that was so damaging during their early years would actually boost their popularity through time. The Rolling Stones have certainly held the test of time and have become a household name. Another aspect that has benefited them is their ability to change (musically) with the times.

Through these long years lots of Rolling Stones memorabilia has been created. Most, however, is merchandise from concerts. It is probable that some Rolling Stone items (other than concert items) from the earlier years exist. But as of this printing no reliable sources have been located or items discovered. The merchandise listed below is a sampling of Rolling Stone items from recent years. It is likely that most items featuring the Stones will be of collectible interest especially when (or if) the group ever disbands.

AIR FRESHNER	1983	MEDO	5-6
COMIC	1990	ROCK FANTASY	3-8
CUP	1990	7-11 Big Gulp 16 oz. promoting TV concert	15-20
GLASSES	1990	promoting tour 3-D type (paper)	20-25
GUITAR		BIG SIX	200-400
GUM CARDS	1965	ABC GUM set of 40 (British)	card 15-20 set 525-700
KEYCHAIN	1983	MUSIDOR	carded 5-10
LIFE MAGAZINE	1971	Stones on cover	10-20
STICKER COLLECTORS ALBUM	1983	J. STANLEY IND.	8-15
STICKERS	1983	MUSIDOR INC. puffy type 4″ x 5 1/2″	5-8 ea.

Comic

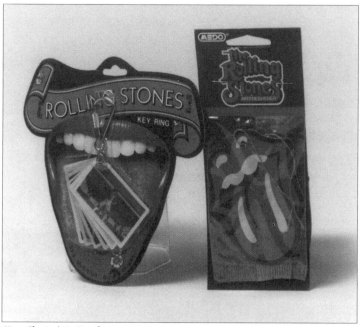

Key Chain/Air Freshener

Sticker Album and Stickers

Cup and Glasses

BOBBY SHERMAN

From 1969-1971 it was nearly impossible to buy a teen magazine without a picture of Bobby Sherman on its cover. A "fav" of a young baby boomer generation, Bobby's blue eyes and teethy smile were every where. Bobby had as much popularity with the young girls who adored him as the young boys who wanted to be like him. Together with a young Donnie Osmond and an aging David Cassidy, Bobby Sherman was certainly a hero to seventies' kids.

With such million selling hits as "Little Woman" and "La La La (If I had you)" Bobby made his way into the pop music scene of the late 1960's. With his growing popularity he became a regular guest on the hip TV show "Shindig." His acting abilities, songs and teen idol status made him an instant fixture to a newly developing bubble gum music generation in both the TV and music industries. Bobby's fame continued bringing more top 40 hits (a total of 7), four of which became gold hits, selling over a million copies.

Bobby also starred as Jeremy Bolt in the popular prime time show "Here Come the Brides," after which he teamed up with another teen star, Wes Stern, in the short lived series "Getting Together". Bobby Sherman's "Groovy" threads made an impact on fashion through the early to mid 1970's. Brightly colored shirts and Bell bottomed pants were a mainstay through this period. You weren't considered "Hip" if you weren't wearing fashions like the teen Idols. The Bradys further reaffirmed this. With eyes on fashion Bobby's Choker necklace, love beads, and peace ring could be purchased through most teen magazines for a dollar or two. These and other items have become highly collectible through the collector's circuit today. The Bobby Sherman lunch box, and especially its thermos have been climbing constantly in value. But it's really the fashion items that say "Bobby Sherman."

FAN CLUB KIT		includes: Record, membership card, mini poster, portraits, booklet, secret decoder, stickers	75-100
GUM CARDS	1972	TOPPS (test) set of 55	card 20-25 set 900-1000 pack 200-225 wrapper 185-200 display box 150-250
LOVE BEADS	1971	Send away	30-50
LUNCH BOX	1972	THERMOS steel	60-100
NECKLACE	1971 1971	"Choker" black suede w/ gold trim. "Peace and Love" (both were sendaways)	40-60 40-60
PAINT AND COLOR ALBUM	1971	ARTCRAFT	25-35
PLAK CARDS	1970	TOPPS (test) set of 35	card 30-50 set 650-725 pack 250-325 wrapper 175-200 display box 225-300
PRIVATE PHOTO ALBUM	1971	Sendaway	35-50
RECORDS		Cut-outs from Rice Krispies ea.	10-15
RING	1971	"Love and Peace" sendaway	20-25
SECRET OF BOBBY SHERMAN	1971	Sendaway (book)	20-25
STICKERS	1971	"Hearts and flowers" sendaway	20-25
THERMOS	1972	THERMOS metal	25-50
TV GUIDE	1971	Bobby on cover	10-20

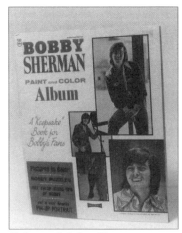

Paint and Color Album

Record

Lunch Box and Thermos

Record

SONNY AND CHER

Fashion was quite possibly Sonny and Cher's most important contribution to the 1960s. Of course, their 1965 hit "I Got You Babe" and nine others didn't hurt them musically. In fact the "Babe" single sold a million copies and fit them right into the (then current) folk rock scene. And fit in is what they did. So much in fact that an entire generation wore Beatle haircuts and dressed like Sonny and Cher. They became a highly publicized, successful act of the 1960s.

Another important aspect of Sonny and Cher is that they were married. For the first time being married (in rock and roll) would be considered hip. During The Beatles' rise to fame John Lennon's first wife was hidden away in a secretive flat so no one would know they were married. It was felt John's popularity might have been threatened. In the long run the family aspect would be important to Rock and Roll by paving the way for such acts as the Partridge Family, Osmonds and the Jackson 5. Love became a fashionable trend and set the tone for the 1960s flower children.

Cher originally wanted to be an actress. Sonny, being 10 years older than Cher, was already a successful songwriter when they married in 1964. In 1971 with their 60' success, Sonny's quick wit and Cher's good looks (and series of top 40s hits) found them on TV for their own very successful show. The Sonny and Cher Comedy Hour made them more popular than ever. The show lasted for several years and was the top- rated variety show of 1973-1974. Their show had subsequent spin offs, none of which was as popular.

Collecting Sonny and Cher memorabilia is both rewarding and profitable. Many of the items marketed relate to Cher and to fashion (of course). Many items can be found today at antique malls and the like. Due to their increasing popularity, both Sonny and Cher items are increasing steadily in value. Condition, as usual, is important since most toy items were boxed. Finding all items in original boxes is always preferable.

DOLLS	1976	MEGO Cher 12″ 6″ x 17″ box	40-60
	1976	MEGO Cher 12″ 4″ x 13″ box	25-40
		O.K.TOYS Cher 12″ bagged	10-15
	1976	MEGO Cher 12″ growing hair	75-125
	1976	MEGO Sonny 12″ 6″ x 17″ box	40-60
DRESSING ROOM	1976	MEGO playset	40-70
MODEL KIT	1968	AMT mustangs	boxed 150-250
MAKE-UP CENTER	1976	MEGO	60-80

Dolls

| **OUTFITS** | 1976 | MEGO Cher carded or boxed | 10-20 |

Cherokee, Cleopatra, Dragon lady, Fortune teller, Frosted feathers, Genie, Good Earth, Gown of Paradise, Half and Half, Hoedown, Image, Indian Squaw, Laverne, Madame Butterfly, Madame Chan, Means Business, Pink Panther, Radiant, Space Princess, Starlight, Steppin out, Strawberry, Sun Kissed, Vagabond, White out,Jumperoo, Easy living, Bolero, Chocolate Mocha, Herky-Jerky, Midnight Blue, Pink Fluff, La Plume, Foxy Lady, Peasant Lady, Eletric Feathers.

| **OUTFITS** | 1976 | MEGO Sonny carded or boxed | 10-20 |

Buckskin, Gypsy King, Hoedown, Private Eye, Space Prince, Tux

THEATER	1976	Cher Theater in the round	50-80
TV GUIDES	1972	Both on cover	each 10-15
	1973	Both on cover	
	1974	Both on cover	
	1975	Cher	
	1976	Both on cover	

TV Guide

Growing Hair Doll

Outfits

Sonny Doll

VANILLA ICE

Suppose you threw a multi-million dollar party and your guests left in three minutes. This is about what happened to Vanilla Ice. He was heralded the Elvis of rap music and within two years' time Vanilla Ice (born Robert Van Winkle) was all but forgotten. With the release of his album "To The Extreme" in 1990 he became almost an overnight sensation. With this instant success came a heavy marketing of memorabilia. But almost as soon as the items appeared in the stores they were in the clearance isle.

Robert got the name Vanilla Ice because he was white (like Vanilla) and like ice, he was cool. He was first noticed when he won a rap contest in Dallas. A record exec. saw his act and offered a record deal. The release of his single "Ice Ice Baby" was to bring him instant success. The single was the first by a white solo rap artist to become a number one pop single. The release of the album followed suit and sold two million copies in a months time. Vanilla Ice was raps first crossover artist.

His early popularity was fueled by touring with such names as M.C. Hammer, ICE-T, and Paula Abdul to name a few.

As a teenager he was involved in motorcross racing, and rapping at friends houses as a hobby. After a bad accident he gave up racing and took up rapping full time. When his career was in its peak he also played a role in one of the popular "Teenage Mutant Ninja Turtles" movies. Musically it can be said that Vanilla Ice was the first really successful white rapper in a predominantly black market. Through the collectible circuit, time has proven that short-lived personalities' merchandise sometimes becomes even more valuable than those who stand the test of time. Vanilla Ice memorabilia falls into this category. Some of these items can still be found at reasonable rates (sometimes in lingering bargain bins) and are worthy of investment. These items should be purchased in the best possible condition. Always buy dolls and microphones in their original boxes. A missing box detracts greatly from an item's value. A box should also be as clean and damage free as possible.

BACK PACKS	1991	ERO 11″ x 16″	each 10-15
BOOK	1991	MODERN PUBL. unauthorized biography	3-5
BUBBLE GUM	1991	TOPPS	each .50-.75
CASSETTES		set of 12 full box of 24 box only	5-10 10-15 3-5
COMIC BOOK	1991	Revolutionary	3-5
DOLLS	1991	THQ 11 1/2″ 3 different	each 20-25
GUM MACHINE ITEMS		capsule w/button gum machine insert	2-3 10-12
RAP GAME	1991	INTERNATIONAL GAMES	20-30
RAP MICROPHONE	1991	THQ	20-25

Bubble Gum Cassettes

Back Packs

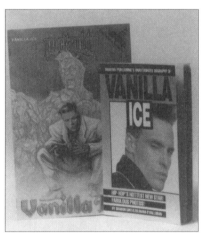

Comic and Book

Dolls

Rap Game

Rap Microphone

MISCELLANEOUS MEMORABILIA ━━━

Through the years almost any rock and roll group that was of any importance has created some sort of memorabilia. Groups with one hit most likely produced a single or in many cases an album. If a group went on tour to promote a single or album, chances are tour books and T-shirts at the very least were produced. These items aren't covered in this book since other books are dedicated soley to this. Many rock bands, due to their popularity with youngsters and teenagers, created items these age groups could relate with. Less popular groups created fewer items. This usually puts their merchandise into a higher value category due to the scarcity, lack of production and/or obscurity of the item.

Some rock groups may have, or continue to, sell out shows everywhere they have been. It's their overall appeal with the younger set that brings out the memorabilia. Some of the best rock and roll collectibles come out of this grouping of miscellaneous items. From ABBA to ZZ Top and most everyone in between are listed. Though many other items quite certainly exist, this chapter's focus is on the most commonly found miscellaneous Rock and Roll items.

ABBA

DOLLS	1978	MATCHBOX 9″ (set of 4)	ea. 50-75

PAULA ABDUL

BUBBLE GUM	1991	Collector folder	2-3
	1991	pack 5″ x 7 1/2″	2-3
	1991	Tin box 2″ x 3 1/2″	3-4
EARRINGS		Play it by ear	5-8
JIGSAW PUZZLE	1990	MILTON BRADLEY (500pcs.)	5-8
SCHOOL FOLDER	1991	ROCK EXPRESS	1-2

FRANKIE AVALON

PILLOW	1950's		50-70

BAY CITY ROLLERS

GUM CARDS	1975	TOPPS	card 1-2
		set of 66	set 60-75
			wax pack 15-20
			wrapper 8-15
			display box 75-85

BEACH BOYS

MODEL KIT	1989	MONOGRAM (lil' douce coupe)	8-12
TV GUIDE	1976		10-15

BLONDIE

CHEW BOPS	1980	Gum shaped record	4-6
MIRROR		9 1/2″ X 12″	10-12
MAGAZINE	1980	FEB. PENTHOUSE (Deborah Harry on cover)	10-15

DEBBIE BOONE

DOLL	1978	MATTEL 11 1/2″	40-65

Debbie Boone: Doll

Boy George: Doll

ABBA: Dolls

Beach Boys: Model Kit

Boy George: Book/Mirror

Blondie: Mirror/Magazine/Chew Bops

Paula Abdul: Bubble Gum Folder/Pack/Tin Box

Paula Abdul: School Folder/Puzzle/Earrings

Shaun Cassidy: Doll

Shaun Cassidy: Guitar

Shaun Cassidy: Jigsaw Puzzle

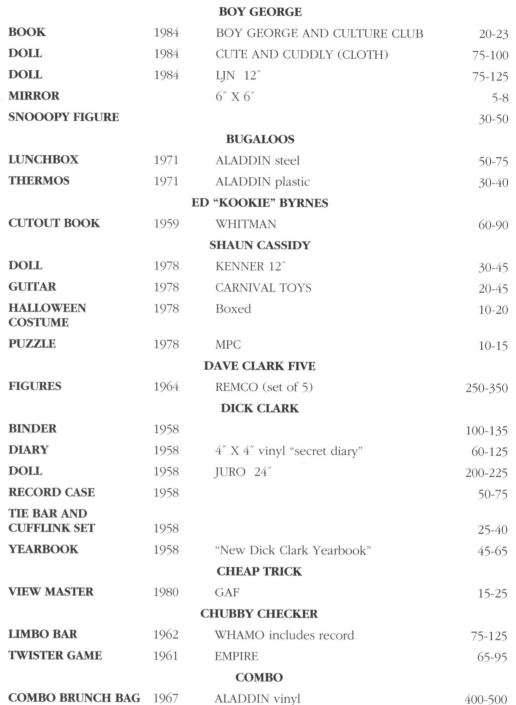

BOY GEORGE

BOOK	1984	BOY GEORGE AND CULTURE CLUB	20-23
DOLL	1984	CUTE AND CUDDLY (CLOTH)	75-100
DOLL	1984	LJN 12″	75-125
MIRROR		6″ X 6″	5-8
SNOOOPY FIGURE			30-50

BUGALOOS

LUNCHBOX	1971	ALADDIN steel	50-75
THERMOS	1971	ALADDIN plastic	30-40

ED "KOOKIE" BYRNES

CUTOUT BOOK	1959	WHITMAN	60-90

SHAUN CASSIDY

DOLL	1978	KENNER 12″	30-45
GUITAR	1978	CARNIVAL TOYS	20-45
HALLOWEEN COSTUME	1978	Boxed	10-20
PUZZLE	1978	MPC	10-15

DAVE CLARK FIVE

FIGURES	1964	REMCO (set of 5)	250-350

DICK CLARK

BINDER	1958		100-135
DIARY	1958	4″ X 4″ vinyl "secret diary"	60-125
DOLL	1958	JURO 24″	200-225
RECORD CASE	1958		50-75
TIE BAR AND CUFFLINK SET	1958		25-40
YEARBOOK	1958	"New Dick Clark Yearbook"	45-65

CHEAP TRICK

VIEW MASTER	1980	GAF	15-25

CHUBBY CHECKER

LIMBO BAR	1962	WHAMO includes record	75-125
TWISTER GAME	1961	EMPIRE	65-95

COMBO

COMBO BRUNCH BAG	1967	ALADDIN vinyl	400-500
THERMOS	1967	steel	50-100

Bugaloos: Lunch Box and Thermos

Dave Clark Five: Doll Set

Disco: Lunch Box and Thermos

Disco Fever: Lunch Box and Thermos

Disco Fever: Ashtray

CULTURE CLUB

BOOK	1983	"In his own words" OMNIBUS	10-20
PUFFY STICKERS	1984	set of 6	10-15

DISCO

LUNCHBOX	1979	ALADDIN steel	35-50
THERMOS	1979	ALADDIN plastic	15-25

DISCO FEVER

ASH TRAY		2″ X 5″ ceramic	15-20
LUNCHBOX	1980	THERMOS steel	40-55
THERMOS	1980	THERMOS plastic	20-30

DARYL DRAGON

DOLL	1977	MEGO 12 3/4″	45-65

DURAN DURAN

BATTERIES	1985	TOSHIBA foreign promo	35-50
GAME	1985	MILTON BRADLEY	40-50
GUM CARDS	1985	TOPPS	card .25-.30
			sticker .40-.50
			set 15-20
			wax pack 2-3
			wrapper .50-1.00
			display box 8-12
MIRROR		6″ X 6″	6-10
SCHOOL FOLDER	1984	BRIGHT IDEAS	8-12

Combo: Brunch Bag and Thermos

Culture Club: Book/ Puffy Stickers

Culture Club: Mug

Daryl Dragon: Doll

Duran Duran: Batteries

Duran Duran: Game

Duran Duran: School Folder/ Mirror/Gum Card Wax Pack

Gloria Estefan: Jigsaw Puzzle

Go Go: Brunch Bag and Thermos

Go Go: Lunch Box and Thermos

Janet Jackson: Jigsaw Puzzle

Journey: Game Cartridge

GLORIA ESTEFAN

JIGSAW PUZZLE	1990	MILTON BRADLEY (100pcs)	3-5

FABIAN

GUM CARDS	1959	TOPPS	card 2-4
		set of 55	set 85-115
			pack 40-55
			wrapper 10-15
			display box 100-150

FABULOUS ROCK RECORDS

GUM PACKS	1968	TOPPS	record 30-40
		set of 16 (Motown stars)	set 450-475
			wrapper 15-20
			display box 150-175

FAME

BEACH TOWEL	1982	FRANCO	20-35
LUNCHBOX	1982	THERMOS plastic	10-15
THERMOS	1982	THERMOS plastic	5-10

FREDDIE AND THE DREAMERS

GUM CARDS	1965	DONRUSS	card 1-2
			set 60-85
			poster 5-8
			wax pack 15-20
			wrapper 5-8
			display box 30-40

JERRY GARCIA

DOLL		CABBAGE PATCH	70-80

GO-GO

BRUNCH BAG	1966	ALADDIN vinyl	175-275
LUNCH BOX	1966	ALADDIN vinyl	150-225
THERMOS	1966	ALADDIN metal	40-55

HEART

BERRET	1987	Bad Animals red felt	30-40

JANET JACKSON

JIGSAW PUZZLE	1991	MILTON BRADLEY	5-8

JOURNEY

GAME CARTRIDGE	1982	ATARI DATA AGE	5-8

Fabian: Gum Cards

Fame: Lunch Box and Thermos/Beach Towel

CYNDI LAUPER

GUM CARDS   1985   card .15-.20
                                                              sticker .30-.35
                        set of 66   set 8-10
                                                              wax pack 2-3
                                                              wrapper .15-.25
                                                              display box 5-8

Mamas and Papas: Show Biz Babies

GARY LEWIS AND THE PLAYBOYS

RECORD   record offer on cereal box   100-150

MAMAS AND THE PAPAS

DOLLS   1967   HASBRO 4 1/2″ (show biz babies)   ea 90-100
MAGAZINE   1967   MARCH. POST group cover   10-12

GEORGE MICHAEL

JIGSAW PUZZLE 1990   MILTON BRADLEY (100pcs.)   3-5
NOTEBOOK   1991   ROCK EXPRESS   3-4
SCHOOL FOLDER 1991   ROCK EXPRESS   1-2

NELSON

BUBBLE GUM   1991   collector folder   3-5
                   1991   pack 5″ x 7 1/2″   3-5
                   1991   tin box 2″ x 3 1/2″   4-6
SCHOOL FOLDER 1991   ROCK EXPRESS   1-2
JIGSAW PUZZLE 1991   MILTON BRADLEY (100pcs.)   3-5

RICK NELSON

LIFE MAGAZINE 1958   DEC. Rick on cover   8-10
PAPER DOLLS   1959   WHITMAN   50-60

Mamas and Papas: Post Magazine

Cyndi Lauper: Gum Cards

George Michael: School Folder/ Jigsaw Puzzle/Notebook

Rick Nelson: Life Magazine

Nelson: Bubble Gum Folder/Bubble Gum Pack/Tin Box

Nelson: Jigsaw Puzzle/School Folder

Prince: School Folder

REO Speedwagon: Plastic Cup

Paul Revere: Coach Model Kit

TV GUIDE	1956	NELSON FAMILY	20-25
		PRINCE	
SCHOOL FOLDER	1984	PLYMOUTH INC.	6-10
		PINK LADY	
DOLL	1974		25-40
LUNCHBOX	1974	ST (foreign group)	800-900
WALLET	1974		25-40
		PUSSYCATS	
LUNCH BOX	1968	ALADDIN vinyl	150-225
THERMOS	1968	ALADDIN metal	35-55
BRUNCH BAG	1968	ALADDIN vinyl	175-240
THERMOS	1968	ALADDIN plastic	25-40
		REO SPEEDWAGON	
PLASTIC CUP		ICEE	5-8
		PAUL REVERE	
COACH MODEL KIT	1967	MPC	275-325
		ROCK ART	
ROCK ART CUPS	1990	TACO BELL full display	30-45
		ROCK CARDS	
ROCK CARDS	1991	BROCKUMS	card .15-.25
		set of 288	sticker .30-.35
		legacy card	ea. 15-20
			set 20-35
		legacy card	set 45-50
			foil pk 1.50-2.00
			hologram set 25-30
			wrapper .25-.30
			poster 5-10
			display box 15-20
ROCK STAR CARDS	1959	NU card set of 64	each 2-4 set 125-150
ROCK STARS CARDS	1979	DONRUSS set of 66	card 1-2 set 50-75 pack 2-4 wrapper 1.50-2.00 display box 15-20

Rock Art: Cup Display   *Pussycats: Brunch Bag & Thermos*   *Pussycats: Lunch Box and Thermos*

DIANA ROSS

DOLLS	1969	IDEAL 18″	250-325
	1977	MEGO 12 3/4″	75-125

SATURDAY NIGHT FEVER

GUM CARDS	1978	DONRUSS	card .25-.30
		set of 66	set 12-15
			pack 2-3
			wrapper 1-2
			display box 8-12
TRASH CAN	1977	P AND K PRODUCTS	50-75

SGT. PEPPERS

GUM CARDS	1978	DONRUSS	card .50-.75
		set of 66	set 20-25
			pack 2-4
			wrapper .50-.75
			display box 5-10

Diana Ross: Mego Doll

SHINDIG

LUNCHBOX	1960'S	RD IND.	150-225

ROD STEWART

JIGSAW PUZZLE	1973	30-40

STYX

MIRROR	12″ X 12″	8-10

SUPER STARS

MUSICARDS	1991	PRO SET	card .20-.30
		set of 260	set 30-35
			pack .75-1.00
			wrapper .20
			display box 3-5

TONI TENNILE

DOLL	1977	MEGO 12 3/4″	35-65

Saturday Night Fever: Trash Can

Shindig: Lunch Box

Styx: Mirror

Super Starts MusiCards Display Box

Tiny Tim: Game

Ritchie Valens: Model Kit

Van Halen: Mirror/Stickers

Toni Tenille: Doll

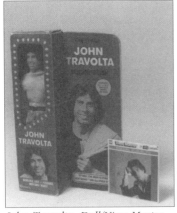

John Travolta: Doll/View Master

John Travolta: Scrapbook

TINY TIM

GAME	1970	PARKER BROS. (of beautiful things)	75-100
TROLL	CA.1967	DAM	40-70

JOHN TRAVOLTA

DOLL	1977	CHEM TOY 12″	20-30
MODEL KIT	1979	REVELL firebird fever	30-40
SCRAPBOOK	1978	SUNRIDGE	5-8
VIEWMASTER	1979	GAF	10-15

RICHIE VALENS

MODEL KIT	1989	MONOGRAM La Bamba model kit	8-12

VAN HALEN

MIRROR	1980s	6″ X 6″	5-8
PUFFY STICKERS	1980s		5-8

VILLAGE PEOPLE

JIGSAW PUZZLE	1978	APC	40-55
VIEWMASTER	1980	GAF	10-15

WILSON PHILLIPS

JIGSAW PUZZLE	1990	MILTON BRADLEY (100pcs.)	3-5

YO-RAPS

GUM CARDS	1991	PRO SET first set 100 second set 50	card .10-.15 set l 15-18 set 2 10-12 pack .75-1.00 wrapper .10-.15 display box 1-2

ZZ TOP

MIRROR	1980s	6″ X 6″	5-8
MODEL KIT	1985	AMT (Eliminator)	20-25
PUZZLE	1980s	In a can	30-40

Wilson Phillips: Puzzle

Village People: Jigsaw Puzzle

Yo Raps: Card Display Box

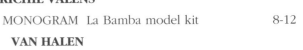

ZZ Top: Mirror

BIBILIOGRAPHY

Encyclopedia of Television Programs
1947-74 Vol I & II
1979 Vincent Terrace A.S. Barnes & Co.

Official Price Guide to Rock and Roll Magazines
Posters and Memorabilia
David Khenkel
1992 Random House

Overstreet Comic Book Guide
Robert Overstreet
1992 Avon Books

Collecting The Beatles
Barbara Fenick
1985 Pierian Press

Price Guide to the Non-Sports Cards
Christopher Benjamin
1992 Edgewater Books

Card Collectors Price Guide
Sept. 1993
Plainview N.J.

Official Price Guide To Memorabilia of
Elvis Presley and The Beatles
Jerry Osborne, Perry Cox, and Joe Lindsay
1988 House of Collectibles

The Billboard Book of Top 40 Hits
Joel Whitburn
1985 Billboard Publications

Life Magazine
Feb. 2, 1959 Time Inc.

ABOUT THE AUTHOR

As a member of The Banana Splits fan club in 1968 Greg's love for music grew. In 1969 he began collecting record albums. With a huge selection of music and a growing appreciation for it, he created "The Music Man" a successful mobile disc-jockey business in the 1980s. In 1986 while attending a toy show with his family, Greg became aware of the vast array of rock and roll collectibles other than records. Soon afterward he bought his first trinket, an Elvis Presley doll. A serious hobby arose from this. Today he collects any rock and roll related items he can find. His collection consists of several thousand rock artifacts. Greg lives with his wife Pam and daughters, Daphne and Tiffany, in Oregon.